Anthony Minghella
Plays: 2

Cigarettes and Chocolate, Hang Up,
What If It's Raining?, Truly, Madly Deeply,
Mosaic, Days Like These

Cigarettes and Chocolate: 'a major state-of-the-nation play about our fragmented lives, our petty infidelities, our adoption of this or that cause and our ultimate indifference to real suffering' *Guardian*

Hang Up: 'intimate, revealing. The words they exchange are commonplace, yet shifted into heightened reality by the suppressed emotions beneath' *The Daily Telegraph*

What If It's Raining?: 'tender but tart dissection of a yuppie marriage on the middle-class rocks . . . incorporates today's prickly sexual tensions and politics into the eternal triangle structure' *City Limits*

Truly, Madly, Deeply is 'about loss, grief and the intense difficulty of renewing a life cruelly narrowed into loneliness . . . Minghella's film creeps up on you unawares and keeps on going unexpected ways' *Guardian*

'Minghella excels in delineating London's multi-national communities of exiles and oddbods. It is rare to find such a tangible sense of place and time in a British film' *The Times*

Anthony Minghella was born on the Isle of Wight of Italian parents. Until 1981 he lectured in Drama at the University of Hull. He was voted Most Promising Playwright by the London Theatre Critics in 1984 and his stage plays include *Whale Music*, *A Little Like Drowning*, *Two Planks and a Passion* and *Made in Bangkok* (London Theatre Critics Best Play of 1986). His television trilogy *What If It's Raining?* was highly acclaimed throughout Europe. Other writing for television includes *Inspector Morse*; *The Storyteller*, a series of nine films for Jim Henson and NBC which won several awards, including an Emmy, a Bafta Award and the Gold Medal at the New York International Film and Television Festival; and *Living With Dinosaurs*, which won an International Emmy in 1991. His BBC radio play *Hang Up* won the Prix Italia in 1988, and *Cigarettes and Chocolate* won the 1989 Giles Cooper Award and 1989 Sony Award. His first film as writer/director, *Truly, Madly, Deeply*, was a great success in Britain and America and won him several prizes, including a Bafta Award and a Writers' Guild Award. *The English*, released in America and the UK in 19__, __ on the novel by Michael Ondaatje, op__ *by Anthony Minghella*

Plays
Whale Music
A Little Like Drowning
Two Planks and A Passion
Made in Bangkok
What If It's Raining?
Hang Up
Cigarettes and Chocolate

Screenplays
Truly, Madly, Deeply
The English Patient

ANTHONY MINGHELLA

Plays: 2

Cigarettes and Chocolate
Hang Up
What If It's Raining?
Truly, Madly, Deeply
Mosaic
Days Like These

with an introduction by the author

Methuen Drama

METHUEN CONTEMPORARY DRAMATISTS

This collection first published in Great Britain 1997
by Methuen Drama

10 9 8 7 6 5 4 3

Methuen Publishing Limited,
215 Vauxhall Bridge Road, London SW1V 1EJ

Cigarettes and Chocolate, Hang Up, What If It's Raining? first published
in 1989 by Methuen Drama, copyright © 1989 by Anthony Minghella
Truly, Madly, Deeply first published in 1991 by Methuen Drama,
copyright © 1991 by Anthony Minghella. 'The Dead Woman' by Pablo
Neruda is published in 'The Captain's Verses' by Pablo Neruda, English
translation Donald D Walsh, A New Directions Paintbook, 1972.
Mosaic and *Days Like These* first published in 1997 by Methuen Drama,
copyright © 1997 by Anthony Minghella

This collection copyright © 1997 by Anthony Minghella
Introduction copyright © 1997 by Anthony Minghella
The author has asserted his moral rights.

A CIP catalogue record for this book
is available from the British Library

ISBN 0 413 71520 5

Typeset in 10/11pt Plantin
by Wilmaset Ltd, Birkenhead, Wirral
Printed in Great Britain
by Cox & Wyman Ltd, Reading Berkshire

Caution

Contents

Anthony Minghella:
A Chronology

Child's Play, Humberside Theatre   1978

Whale Music, Leicester Haymarket Granada TV
film 1983, and BBC Radio 4, 1985   1981

A Little Like Drowning, CV-One Touring
Company and BBC Radio 4, 1989   1982

Two Planks and A Passion, Northcott Theatre,
and BBC Radio 3, 1986   1983

Love Bites, Derby Playhouse   1984

Made in Bangkok, Aldwych Theatre, London   1986

What If It's Raining?, Limehouse/Channel 4 TV   1986

The Storyteller, Jim Henson Productions/NBC/
TVS/Channel 4 TV   1987

Hang Up, London Contemporary Dance Theatre
and BBC Radio 3, 1987   1987

Cigarettes and Chocolate, BBC Radio 4   1988

Living with Dinosaurs, Jim Henson Productions/
NBC/TVS/Channel 4 TV   1989

The Mathematics of a Kiss, short opera with
Orlando Gough and John Lunn for Signals/
Dancelines/Channel 4 TV   1989

Days Like These, short monologue for Comic
Relief   1989

Second Thoughts, for Mel Smith and Griff Rhys
Jones in *Small Doses*, Talkback/BBC TV   1989

Author's Note

I've never been much interested or concerned with adjudicating the behaviour of individuals. It has always seemed clear to me that behaviour is primarily a reflection, albeit distorted, of society's messages to its people. I don't sense this in any dark, conspiratorial sense; simply if we collectively opt for the misanthropic, that's what we must surely get back. So nothing which happens in the rooms of these plays makes sense without the activity outside of their windows.

The characters in this volume can't communicate with each other, are often unfaithful or unhappy or lost, and united in their search to give meaning to their lives through careers, through acquisitions, through art, through philanthropy, through therapy, through affairs, through silence. They are increasingly cluttered. And spiritually bankrupt. The writing is not so much satirical as disappointed and impatient, both with its material and itself. For these plays are as much a mirror held up to my own choices as they are a reflection of the society in which I found myself in a five year period between 1987 and 1991. To borrow from Wilde, we lived then, and still do, in a time which knows the price of everything but the value of nothing. And yet, amidst these accounts of failure of one kind or another, there is a yearning for something better, more decent – but not, perhaps, more civilised. The recurring weaknesses of human beings seem to me to be leavened by the potential for good, for laughter, for boundless generosity, for healing. And, for love.

Anthony Minghella
London, January 1997.

Acknowledgements

My thanks to the rosary of names listed with each text. They each helped fashion the productions as they came to be seen or heard. If nothing else, these plays and screenplays are a testimony to the virtues of maintaining working relationships and professional friendships. Appropriately, triple thanks to the repeated names: my friends and colleagues, Robert Cooper, Mark Shivas, Michael Maloney and Jonathan Lunn; and, in particular, to Juliet Stevenson, brilliant actress, brilliant accomplice, who would dignify my slightest line and has frequently done so.

Cigarettes and Chocolate was commissioned by John Tydeman and Gordon House as part of BBC Radio's *Globe Theatre Season.*

Hang Up was commissioned by the choreographer, Jonathan Lunn, to accompany a duet for himself and Lauren Potter for London Contemporary Dance Theatre. The play was subsequently broadcast on Radio 3 through the enterprise of Robert Cooper.

What If It's Raining? was commissioned by Granada Television, and despite the efforts of June Howson and Howard Baker, seemed in danger of becoming marooned there. I am much indebted to Louise Cooper for her perseverance in placing the trilogy long after my own efforts had dimmed, to David Benedictus, then Commissioning Editor at Channel 4, for his role in fostering the project; and to the Producer, Mark Shivas, for steering me through.

Truly, Madly, Deeply was commissioned by Robert Cooper as a BBC film and written for Juliet Stevenson.

Mosaic was written for another duet by Jonathan Lunn, this time as part of BBC2's *Dancelines* series

Days Like These was written for *Comic Relief* and owes much to Richard Curtis and Paul Weiland.

There is a list
and it says
this person for doing this
and that person for doing nothing
and this person for not howling in rage
and that for desperately hanging on to the reasons the reasons
and
there is an avenger
who would be left?

from *In the Heart of the Beast* C. K. Williams

Cigarettes
and Chocolate

for Kenny McBain 1946–89

'I want it to go silent, it wants to go silent, it can't, it
does for a second, then it starts again, that's not the real
silence, it says that's not the real silence, what can be
said of the real silence, I don't know . . .'

The Unnameable, Samuel Beckett

Cigarettes and Chocolate was first broadcast by BBC Radio 4 in November 1988, with the following cast:

Gemma	Jenny Howe
Rob	Bill Nighy
Lorna	Juliet Stevenson
Alistair	Alex Norton
Mother	Joan Campion
Gail	Jane Gurnett
Sample	Christopher Ravenscroft
Concepcion	Sally Eldridge

Directed by Robert Cooper and Anthony Minghella

Telephone ringing.

Gemma (*a taped answerphone message*) Hello, you've rung 341 6293. If you'd like to leave a message for Gemma, please do so after you hear the tone.

Tone. Then **Gemma**'s *messages are heard.*

Rob It's me. Listen, did I leave my new toothbrush with you? The one with the, it's got a, you know, the big head . . . I think it was in your bag for some reason. Don't brush your hair with it. And don't open the olive oil, I need something to give my sister. Can I come round later for sex?

Tone.

Lorna Hi, it's me, are we on for tonight? Will you ring me before we meet and remind me to bring my glasses, because I can't read the subtitles without them. Two reviews are in favour, one against. Ring at seven, six forty-five, and say glasses. Ta ra.

Tone.

Rob It's Rob. I'm leaving home for the office, and I don't know what time I'll be home, late possibly, probably, probably ridiculously late. Best thing would be to stay with you otherwise I'll have to drive the extra seven hundred yards to my flat. Take pity on me.

Tone.

Alistair Gemma, look it's Alistair, you know, if you had anything from me this morning, you know, like a letter, don't read it, you know, if you haven't already opened, and if you have, if you have, if you have, don't think of it as a problem, you know, think of it as a not very good poem . . .

Tone.

Mother (*sceptical*) Gemma? It's your mother. Are you there? If you're there and not answering can you pick up the telephone? Gemma? I suppose you're out. Could you please telephone when you get in.

Tone.

Rob   Rob. Two-thirty. I'm at work. Call me.

Tone.

Gail (*torrential*)   Gemma, it's Gail. I hoped you'd be in because I wanted you to come and look at a flat with me. I'll read you the details, I can never remember whether your machine cuts you off after thirty seconds, I hope not because that drives me crazy, anyway, listen it's in, well the postcode is N19 but it's really Highgate Borders, I mean the Agents say Highgate which it isn't, but it's not inconvenient and anyway Highgate's ridiculous, as bad as you, it's impossible and this place has got a garden, it says pretty west-facing garden, although it doesn't say a length which is a bad sign, yesterday I saw a place in Camden with a Nice Town Garden, this is true, the details said Nice Town Garden and there was nothing, there wasn't one. There was a back yard where this guy had his bicycle and even that wouldn't stand straight, it was sort of bent up to squeeze it in.

Cut off tone.

Me again. I hate it when that happens. It makes you feel terrible, terribly rejecting, where was I? It's in Hornsey, did I say that, but I measured in the *A-Z* and it's really no further than, it's not as far north as Muswell Hill, say . . . it's about two inches above the Post Office Tower. I can't stand Muswell Hill. I hate the architecture as much as anything else: all those porches and it's smug, it's got smug porches. Will you come and look at this place with me? Two bedrooms, plus a bedroom/study so there's room for the baby, there'll be room for the baby, plus the garden as I said . . . reception: fireplace, cornices, 16′ x 11′ which is okay, and dado rails, dado rails, (*Pronounces the 'A' differently, first as in baby then as in far, then sing-song to the tune of 'Let's Call the Whole Thing Off'.)* You say Dado and I say Dado, whichever it is, who cares, so, I must hurry before I get cut off . . . I've got a scan at three tomorrow and I could go straight from that, so will you phone and let me know yes or no so I can make the appointment? It's much easier when you've got someone with, and Sample has a horror . . . actually if I could choose you'd come with me for the scan as well, would you hate

Cut off tone.

Lorna It's Lorna, Gem, where are you? I'm in a callbox opposite the cinema. Are you on your way? Well, I'm assuming you're on your way. If for any reason you haven't left, I'll leave your ticket at the Box Office, or should I wait? There's a queue, Gem, and it's starting, what do I do? Just hurry up, will you!

Tone.

Rob It's Rob.

Tone.

Rob *sighs, puts the phone down.*

Tone.

Gemma's *flat. Morning.*

We hear the sounds of a spring morning in England. Larks, grasshoppers. Music begins, opening bars from Bach's 'Matthew Passion'. But we might feel we're hearing it through open french windows, because **Gemma** *is speaking from her small, walled garden in North London.*

Gemma The day I stopped talking was one of those perfect days we have in England. They come in the spring and in the autumn, differently, the one full of

entrance the other full of exit, but the same in the way
the air thins and you can see the edge of everything.
And somehow green is more green, blue more blue. I
wish I'd had another week, but there it was, a big red
cross on my calendar, and everything was ready . . . I'd
had my holiday, in Italy, wonderful, wonderful, as if I'd
put my tongue on a small pile of salt . . . or a glass of
wine. Italy was a glass of dark wine swilled in the
mouth. And I'd spoken to them all, in return, carefully,
loving them all, like suicide in a way: to stop talking.
Like killing oneself.

Music and garden out.

Interior, cafe, day time.

Cafe with sophisticated background music, jazz or similar.

Rob   Hi, have you been waiting?

Lorna   No.

Rob   Am I always late?

Lorna   I think so, yes.

Rob   Yes, I think I am. Not very good is it?

Lorna   I adjust. Your coffee's cold. Actually, I don't
think you were late in the beginning.

Rob   You look nice. I'm supposed to be at a meeting.

Lorna   Really, and what? What? Do you mean – ?

Rob   I'm not going. I made some excuse. Sod it.

Lorna   What? You were meeting your lover?

Rob   Exactly. That's exactly what I said.

Lorna   I can believe that.

Rob   Lorna, she's stopped talking.

Lorna   What? Who?

Rob Gemma! She's not talking. I went there this morning and she had just ceased to talk, she won't answer the telephone, she won't return calls, she won't say a single word to me.

Lorna Why?

Rob Well, obviously, because of this . . .

Lorna Why? Did you tell her?

Rob No.

Lorna Well I certainly haven't told her.

Rob She's very intuitive, she's very acute about these things.

Lorna Really? I wouldn't have said so.

Rob I'm telling you.

Lorna I've just been on holiday with you both and we managed to –

Rob There's no need to –

Lorna I'm not being anything, I'm just pointing out –

Rob I didn't say you were being anything – anyway, let's –

Lorna Would you rather we stopped seeing each other?

Rob No.

Lorna What then?

Gail Rob!

Rob Gail! Hi! Hi! Lorna and I are having an assignation! Ignore us!

Gail Oh hi, Lorna, I didn't realise it was you, wonderful coat, is that new? Where's Tom?

Lorna It's ancient, it is nice though, isn't it? Sit down. Tom's with Gerti. (*The Nanny.*) Have you met Gerti?

Gail   I thought it was Anna?

Lorna   No, Anna's gone. Gerti's wonderful.

Gail   Can she speak English?

Lorna   She's Danish. She speaks better English than me.

Rob   Have some coffee.

Gail   I thought you were off coffee for Lent?

Rob   This is mostly froth.

Lorna   Have some froth. You look wonderful.

Gail   Thanks. I've put on fourteen-and-a-half pounds.

Rob (*to the* **Waitress**)   Excuse me, could we have another coffee? Actually, I'll have another, make it three could you? Cappucino. Thanks a lot.

Gail   Any more I'm going to have to make bras out of duffle bags.

Lorna   Is it going well?

Gail   Apparently. The amniocentesis was, you know, clear.

Lorna   Terrific. So do you know what sex it is?

Gail   I do, Lorna, but I've got to keep it a secret. Sample doesn't want to know.

Lorna   Right.

Gail   How's Stephen? What are you two doing here? Is this really an assignation?

Rob   Seriously.

Gail   How exciting. Is a threesome out of the question?

Rob   Jump in.

Gail   How's Gemma?

Rob   She's great.

Gail   She doesn't ring back when you leave a message on that bloody machine. What's the matter with her, the old bag? I wanted her to come and look at some places with me. I've only discovered this cafe since I've been flat-hunting. It's really nice, isn't it?

Rob   Yeah.

Gail   I know what I wanted to ask you, Lorna . . . (*Deflected.*) Look at you both, I forgot you were all in Italy together, look at you, it's not the coat, well it is the coat, but it's the colour . . . it's February and you've both caught the sun! Was it wonderful?

Rob   It was. Tom was wonderful. The grown-ups were okay. Stephen cheated at Scrabble.

Lorna   So did you.

Rob   I cheated openly. Stephen pretended he wasn't. I always cheat. If you always cheat, it's hardly cheating at all, is the way I look at it.

Gail   Did Gemma have a good time? Oh God, you pigs, I love Italy.

Lorna   Gemma was fine. Political.

Rob   She wasn't political.

Lorna   She wanted to adopt a Vietnamese baby we saw outside the Uffizi.

Gail   Why?

Lorna   Why, Rob?

Rob   That's not fair. The context was . . . that's not fair, Lorna. It was because we were having such a good time.

Gail   I'm having a nice time I think I'll adopt that Vietnamese boy? Was he up for sale?

Rob   No. No, of course not. No, he had Dutch parents. At least we assumed they were Dutch. They wore those funny shoes that you can get in Covent

Garden: so ugly you can convince yourself they're good for you. Only Dutch people wear them.

Gail   You mean clogs?

Rob   Not clogs. Those shoes which look like somebody ran over a pair of Nature Treks. And they had this Vietnamese boy, extraordinarily beautiful. (*Consulting* **Lorna**.) Wasn't he? (*To the* **Waitress** *who's arrived with the coffees*.) Thanks. Do you want anything else, Gail? We could get you up to fifteen pounds if you're interested.

Lorna   I'm going to have to get my skates on shortly.

Rob   Really? Should I cancel the hotel room?

Lorna (*saying 'Yes'*)   Sorry.

Gail   I'm completely confused about this Dutch Vietnamese boy.

Rob   Ask Gemma. It was her idea. She just said, actually she didn't just say – she went on about it all night. Did I tell you this, Lorna? You know we carried on the conversation the entire night? She kept saying 'How much do we give back? Expressed as a percentage of what we have: how much do we give back?'

Gemma's *flat. Evening. Bach's 'Matthew Passion'.*

Alistair   Oh God, Gemma, I feel terrible now, I'm going to have to tell the others, I'm going to have to tell Rob, I'm going to get my wee nose bloodied, this love I have for you, this love I mentioned in my letter, it's not a big obstacle type of love, it's not a trip over me on your front doorstep type of love, it's not a, it's small, it's a kind of very irrelevant passion, it was hardly worth writing down, it started off as a p.s. and got bigger in the letter, I'm speaking of proportion, I love you in brackets is what I was saying, oh-by-the-way type of thing; on a scale of one to ten, you know: one-

and-a-half when I'm feeling really badly about it, it's a
hot water bottle, 'I'm feeling terrible but at least
Alistair loves me', when the fellow walks out on you,
'You're by yourself Gemma but at least that little
chappie nurses a crushette I can cry on his shoulder
while I wait for Mr Right to come along' it was not,
repeat not, block capitals IT WAS NOT INTENDED
TO MAKE YOU STOP TALKING TO
EVERYONE! Oh God, Gemma.

A Restaurant. Day.

Rob Italy. Italy was the trouble, was where it started,
I realise that now, this wonderful restaurant we kept
going to, we went with Stephen and Lorna and Tom
who's their, who's two or something, well you know
Tom anyway . . . Sample, have I told you this?

Sample I don't think so, was this when – ?

Rob (*ploughing on*) The food was, God, the first time
we went they brought, there was no menu, they just
brought food to the table . . . – *do you want these
mushrooms? Fantastic wild mushrooms,* – and there was
fish, really fresh, these people were terrific, we kept
going back, you could see the river from the table, oh
God, it was a great holiday. Gemma was, she had the
best time, we were talking about kids, she kept holding
Tom and, who's really nice, in as much as a two-year-
old, although they, Stephen's always making him wear
these ridiculous, but he's remarkable, in the restaurant,
perfect, of course that's the Italians they make you feel
as if anything is perfectly, so no, and then she
(*Distracted suddenly.*) Do you notice the central heating?

Sample I don't know. I'm not cold. Are you cold?

Rob No. No. I'm hot. I'm too hot. Is it on?

Sample I expect so. It's February. I expect it's on.
Feel the radiator. It's just behind you.

Rob   Well it isn't on. As it happens. I don't know, but there's vestigial central heating, do you know what I mean? The plants. The plants here are dying of it, and they're just plants, imagine what it's doing to us, I really noticed that when we came back here, of course the first thing you notice is the traffic which is now ridiculous, it is ridiculous, imagine a Martian . . . the traffic, the streets, I think that must be a strike, I'm sure it's not absence which had made them so dirty, not my absence, our absence, but the absence of street cleaners. My flat when I got back, outside, – you know the place outside where we leave the rubbish – so you arrive and wade through the armadas of black bags, well there's somebody who lives in the flats who clearly has psychopathic tendencies, really, during the election somebody delivered a Labour Party car sticker and it was in my letter box, you know where the letter rack is, with the dominoes, you know where the dominoes are . . .

Sample (*he does*)   I love that, was that your idea?

Rob   It might have been the psychopath who used the dominoes, must have been when I came to think of it, you have to have a psychopathic turn of mind to use dominoes to number the letter boxes, so anyway I get home in the evening and the sticker is still there in my letter box, except now it's in a thousand little pieces, literally, thousands of little pieces, which is psychopathic.

Sample (*agreeing*)   God. (*Pause.*) Gemma hates your flat, doesn't she, because of that, because she said the people who live there, the other people, she's always saying that, the Porsches . . .

Rob (*irritated*)   There's only one Porsche, the secretary of the Labour Party lives there as well as it happens, she's always doing that . . . there's only one Porsche in the entire building. It's a left-hand drive, it's an old left-hand drive Porsche, it's actually rather beautiful. Of course it's revolting. It's full of revolting people. You know, but it's very beautiful, and it's got the park. When you've been somewhere healthy you really appreciate that, somewhere sane, even fresh air, even that is no longer freely available. Even that's political. My point is, about the flat, my flat, is that with this strike, I'm assuming it is a strike, instead of being careful, the psychopath has lost all self-control and has abandoned the black bag regime . . . you know they won't take the rubbish unless it's in black bags? Well that's all out of the window and there's this kind of deluge of little shopping bags, plastic carrier bags with stuff spilling out, bits of pizza and God knows what, the guy clearly is the Take Away king of North London, when they catch him there will be serious economic problems in the Indian Restaurant trade, and it's all there, the evidence, and each time I get home I want to kill him, I want to wade in to his little plastic bags and discover his name, I know somewhere between the polystyrene and foil containers, between the Chicken Tikka Masala and the, I'm sure there's abandoned pornography as well, stuff which is delivered in plain brown envelopes, there are a lot of bits of plain brown envelopes and stuff from American Express, there will be his name, he will have left his name somewhere on an envelope, and once I've found it I intend to scoop up an armful of this crap which is now blocking the entrance to the flats, you have to climb over it, you have to queue up with the vermin, the cockroaches, the queues of parasites who are racing up the hill to the feast, I am going to scoop up the worst of this crap and ring his bell and dump it over his mentally deranged psychopathic little head.

Sample That's awful. Because it's a beautiful flat.

Rob I know, I'm really lucky, I'm really blessed to have it. I feel terrible. All my friends come round, this is my paranoia, my friends come round and they think sod him.

Sample I always think that. I think sod him for having such a terrific flat.

Rob Except Gemma. Who hates it.

Sample Well, I expect she means the windows. Because there aren't really any windows.

Rob (*raging*) Of course there are windows! There are loads of windows!

Sample (*conciliatory*) I suppose she – I love it, I keep telling you, I love it, I'll swap – but you know she loves light.

Rob I love light! This makes me really angry. She doesn't have copyright on liking light. Light is very important to me, and my flat is often very light, but she does this, she makes a decision about something and that's it, finished, my flat has no light and is full of Porsches. If she'd agree to live with me, which after all this time is one of the more tired jokes among our friends, right? If she'd move in with me we could buy somewhere really special which was all windows if that is what she wants, we could buy a huge greenhouse and make babies, Vietnamese babies if that's what she wants, that's another thing I have to tell you about, the Vietnamese baby . . . Christ . . . her place is not that light as it happens and it's damp and then she has the central heating, this is my point, this is what I was saying just now . . . she has the central heating up full blast and then everyone feels ill all the time. Since we got back from Italy I have felt ill, physically ill, all the time, which is what's wrong with her, probably, something as simple as the central heating and instead of turning it down, turning it off, or agreeing to buy a flat with me, she has this whatever it is, this . . . what do you think it is? I don't know. She won't speak to me. Has she spoken to you? She hasn't spoken to anyone. Has she said anything to you? Has she said anything to Gail?

Sample   Nothing. No. I don't think so.

Rob   Well, if she does: tell her to turn the central heating off. Sample, honestly, she has not said a word to anyone for a week. I mean, it's ridiculous. Now she's turned her machine off. The phone just rings and rings.

Phone ringing and ringing.

Gemma's *flat. Evening.*

Gail *with* **Gemma**, *music. Bach's 'Matthew Passion'.*

Gail   Sample says I'm to mention the central heating to you although I can't think why, it's not on is it? Is it because there's something wrong with your central heating and because you're not speaking you can't do anything about it? Why don't you write down something on a piece of paper? That wouldn't compromise you would it? Is it a love affair? Who is it? Or is Rob fooling around? I have to tell you Lorna and I and Sample spent an entire evening on Friday speculating, your ears must have been burning! It's a great way to become the centre of attention, that's my problem I talk too much and then nobody's interested, although I think you could say a few words and still be mysterious, if it's a bit of mystery you're after. Anyway, for the record: I thought you were having an affair, Lorna thought it was Rob, I mean something to do with Rob, – I'm trying to read your face, Gem, you're so inscrutable! It's not the baby, is it? It's not my baby, is it? (*She thinks it might be.*) I don't think it is. I can't think it could be that. I know you – I know that's something you'd eventually, but, (*doesn't pursue it.*) I can't remember what Sample thought, if indeed he did think, impending fatherhood is making him all sort of fey and gloomy and concerned, I can't get him to come anywhere near me, he's gone all reverent which is a bit ridiculous, I think he's given me up for Lent, I'm only eighteen weeks. Anyway I know you think I'm too

smutty, to tell you the truth, Gem, it'll be quite nice
not to feel obliged to every five minutes; I mean enough
is enough, particularly if you're sort of saying we'll be
doing this for donkey's years. It's like serving up
spaghetti bolognese every night. Who needs it? I mean I
like my spag. bol. as much as the next girl, that is not
my point, this is what I was trying to say to Sample last
night, I don't know how it started as he's even started
coming to bed in track suit bottoms, but probably
because I said something like 'this is nice holding
hands', which'll teach me for not saying what I thought
which was, you know, 'I won't break', but he said
something like 'I hope you don't like it more than our
wild nights of passion,' Well! apart from I imagine your
finding it as tricky as I do to imagine Sample in a wild
night of anything, he can be very sweet to me, I mean
for God's sake I love the bloke, I'm having his baby, so
the point is last night he starts sulking right after I've
lied about liking holding hands with him in his track
suit bottoms and me in my sleep bra and so he starts
this huge sulk about us never doing it ever again
because he's got the calendar out by this time and is
sort of saying well it's at least five months after this and
ten weeks after that and stitches, which of course puts
the fear of God up me and before you know it we're
both really miserable but to tell you the truth I'm quite
relieved because it means, I mean do you know
anybody, any woman, who deep down, I mean really
deep down under the first deep down where you admit
to being insatiably lustful about everybody, what I'm
saying is under that layer have you met anybody who
actually would rather, I mean I'm not saying to begin
with then you're courting and sorting out whether or
not he fancies you, he's got to not be able to keep his
hands off you at that stage, then that's fine: up the
stairs, in the back of the Renault, every five minutes, I
mean great, that's sort of required, but once you've said
to yourself 'okay you'll do' well it's what I said about
the old spag. bol. isn't it? See! if you don't shut me up

look what happens! Tell you the truth, Gem, I'm
getting a bit worked up about this baby, it's the
hormones, obviously, look, these are all new, I never
had a mark on my face, that's one thing I've always had
is my skin, Gem, you know I may not be a beauty but
I've always had fantastic skin, that's not vanity, and
now suddenly look at all that and I just know I'm going
to have stretch marks like a deflated balloon, which is
fine, but that's always been my strong point, Gem, you
know so it seems bloody unfair, but that's not it
anyway, it's just I've been pregnant before, right, so
now I've said, oh shit, not a big deal I have been
pregnant before, I expect if the chips were down I'm
not alone in this, which is neither here nor there, you
know I'm not one of those women who, (*she's crying.*)
you know I was speaking to this American woman the
other day who has got everything, pool in the garden,
holidays in Hawaii and she kept saying – you don't
know her, it's got nothing to do with a swimming pool,
she kept saying 'fill your house up with babies, Gail, fill
your house with babies, like flowers . . .', great, I
haven't even got a flat yet, and if I do I'll fill it with
myself and – because Sample won't live there, will he? I
mean he's never wanted to live with me before, so . . .
I'm just saying the abortion thing which I'd do again if
it were the same circumstances because I was like a kid
at the time myself, I mean I wasn't a kid according to
my passport, but in every other respect and the guy
would have run a mile, of course, which all just goes to
making this baby very important, because I can feel it
and it feels like a big sob in my stomach, all day I keep
thinking it's there like this great sobbing in my stomach
. . . fill your house with babies, like flowers . . . I think
you should say something, Gemma, because it's not fair
is it, all these confessions, I bet you're getting all these
wonderful confessions, is there a tape recorder? Have
you seen the size of my tits? Pretty impressive, eh?
Anyway, I've passed on the stuff about the central
heating. Do you think anybody could survive in

Holloway, I mean off the Holloway Road? I don't think
so. (*Bleak.*) Actually, it's bloody awful.

The music plays.

Soho Office. Day.

Alistair's *office.* **Alistair** *and* **Rob**

Rob   How could anyone so beautiful do that to
himself? I swear, Al. That is what she said. Those were
her words. Such a beautiful face. How could he set fire
to himself? I have to say it made me pretty angry.

Alistair   What? That the monk was beautiful?

Rob   No, come on: Gemma. Come on. I got angry
with her, because there we were, the entire day
poisoned, and I thought well okay, this monk has done
this to himself and he felt that was important.
Obviously, I mean, obviously he felt it was crucial or
something, it was obviously not just a gesture, and so
fine it screws up all our plans and we send everybody
home, including my sister who already thinks Gem is,
and okay it's important, but then she says such a
beautiful face and I'm afraid that made me furious. And
she's got him up on her noticeboard, the beautiful self-
immolator, and frankly, Alistair, I almost burned his
photograph with my lighter.

Alistair   Why? I don't follow. Because she thought he
was beautiful? Sorry Rob, I don't follow you.

Rob   I'm just saying we're talking about a woman who
went to Greenham Common, okay, which is fine by me,
great, but she has to drive back here and find out where
Greenham Common is on the map. That's all.

Alistair   And?

Rob   Well, you know, if you're going to have

principles, Alistair, buy yourself a map and a noticeboard.

Alistair   If I'm getting your gist you're complaining because Gemma didn't know where Greenham Common was before she went there, or that she was upset when a beautiful monk committed suicide because of what was happening in Tibet . . . am I right, pal? I mean she knew Greenham Common was in England. That would do for me. Or do you need a woman with Geography 'A' Level?

Rob   And what's all this about? The silence? I mean what is all that about?

Alistair (*thrown*)   I don't know, Rob. I mean if you don't know. (*Shrugs.*) I don't know.

Rob   Italy. Italy must have something to do with it. And the Vietnamese baby. Who was probably Dutch. (*Despairing.*) You know. I can't go round there, Alistair. I can't bear all that music. The 'Matthew Passion'. I keep thinking it must be a clue. Have you been round? Does your ioniser have any effect do you think? I lie in my room with mine in my mouth. You can get tiny electric shocks on the tongue.

Alistair   You should talk to Concepcion.

Rob   Should I? Who's Concepcion? I thought your cleaner was called Concepcion?

Alistair   That's right. She's my cleaner. She's terrific. She's a psychiatrist.

Rob   Great. What? You mean she has insight and stuff? You talk to her? What are you talking about, Alistair?

Alistair   I just said, she's a psychiatrist. She trained as a psychiatrist in Argentina. She's only a cleaner in London. In Argentina she's a psychiatrist.

Rob   Your cleaner is a psychiatrist.

Alistair That's right. I've told you before, actually.
She's amazing. I get my shirts ironed by an amazingly
beautiful Argentinian psychiatrist.

Rob Listen, would you mind if I opened the window,
I find it difficult to breathe in here, do you notice that?
I think it's just very stuffy at the moment. How can you
work in here with all these dead plants? (*Opens window
to a deluge of traffic.*) I got clamped this morning. You
can't drive off. Nothing happens. I thought I'd just
drive off with that notice in front of my face, on the
three wheels. But you can't. It is pointless driving in
London. There is absolutely no point. There is a man
directly below your office in a very big car and because
the traffic has clearly unhinged him, he is stuck
sideways across the road. His nose is touching a parked
BMW and his tail is touching another parked BMW. In
about two sec – the blue BMW has a dent . . . and now
so does the black one . . . (*We hear the appropriate
clunks and thuds and engine chorus.*)
blue 2 black 1
blue 3 black 1
blue 3 black 2
(*Car squeals off.*) and off to the gym, to the T'ai Chi, to
the aromatherapy, to the . . .

Alistair No, I've got this great deal going with
Concepcion because I'm paying her three fifty an hour
right? Which is not cheap but is the going rate for
domestic help, so fine, but thrown in I get a little
therapy, it's limited vocabulary therapy, but I get to
talk over the vacuum cleaner or the washing machine, I
feel everything's being tidied up at once. It's a
wonderful deal. I've made all sorts of discoveries.

Rob Such as?

Alistair Such as the vaccuum cleaner whistles when
the bag is full, such as you put a tennis ball in the
washing machine for some obscure but deeply helpful
reason, such as I harbour this desire to murder my

cousin. Which was not a discovery but I've owned up to it. No, Concepcion is perfect, or would be if she would sleep with me.

Rob Sounds great. Which cousin?

Alistair Such as I am in love with Gemma.

Rob She told you this, or you told her?

Alistair I'm serious, Rob. I wrote to Gemma and told her. I had to. I know it's not how you treat your mates, but this was serious. I wrote her a letter, not a big deal or anything, you know, in the third paragraph of this wee note, and next thing she's not speaking to anyone.

Rob Alistair, only you and your psychiatric cleaner didn't know you were in love with Gemma, it's got nothing to do with your letter. I don't mean to belittle the depth of feeling and, but it has nothing to do with this confession.

Alistair Right.

Rob Because Gemma knew, is what I am saying. She knew. You wear it on your sleeve, you come to dinner and it's 'Could you pass the wine, Gemma, and I'm in love with you.' 'Oh Gemma, do you really think so and I'm in love with you.' 'Gemma, fantastic kidney beans and I'm in love with you'. So listen: don't feel badly because it's fine, Alistair, really, and I'm delighted you're in love with her, it made her feel nice, I'm sure it still does, she's probably a little bit in love with you.

Alistair Yeah, but you know Rob I really love her. Oh God. I cried when I told Concepcion. Oh God, it was just the relief of admitting it. I think I'm going to cry again now which would be embarrassing, I am not famous in this office for laughing on the wrong side of my face as my dad would say. Don't laugh on the wrong side of your face, son. Oh.

Gemma's *flat. Evening.*

The 'Matthew Passion'.

Rob   I am actually very aggravated, you know. I find
it very aggravating. I find it childish, I find it shocking
and aggressive, very aggressive, actually, because you
know what it says to me Gem
because by all means don't speak to the world,
go right ahead.
but with me, it says, I include you with the
others, I exclude you from anything private,
or intimate or
plus, I'm pretty certain I know what, why,
what's behind all of this, and I feel like
I'm being put in the stocks for it
so, if there is a problem, instead of talking about it
you

The music plays.

I don't know if you're eating, or sleeping
I don't know what you're thinking.

The music plays.

Rob *is suddenly agitated.*

what?
and please don't stare at that bloody
photograph!
because you know I have a particular
antipathy towards that picture, we've been
through this.
I don't think it's very clever, or brave, or
effective, or real, or real! to set fire to
yourself,
in fact, it's very similar,
what you're doing, what he's doing.
it's very similar,
it's like a kind of major sulk, isn't it?

in fact, I am going to burn that picture,
I should have done this the last time,

*He rips the photograph off the notice board
holds it up threateningly –*

well talk to me then, talk to me, talk to me

Pause.

okay.
okay.

He sets fire to the photograph with his lighter.

this is just so . . .

It burns.

sod it
look, I'll get you another picture, I shouldn't have
done that.
I shouldn't have done that
you know, but I'm frustrated. I'll find the photograph
and get you another one.
I'm sorry, I shouldn't have done that.
Look, I'll go.

Pause.
The music plays, **Rob** *sighs.*

Gemma.

The music plays.

Gemma?

The music plays.

Gemma's *flat. Morning. The 'Matthew Passion'.*

Alistair *and* **Gemma** *are listening. The work finishes.
We hear applause.*

Alistair   No, I like it. I'm really getting to like it.

*The recording starts again. Side one of a piece which is
very, very long.*

Alistair (*taking a deep breath. The price of
love*)   Again? Great. Great.

He hums and half sings.

Alistair   Terrific.

Alistair's *flat. Day.*

Rob *to* **Concepcion. Concepcion** *is ironing.*

Rob   Is it . . . do you mind if . . . I . . . I should have
brought my shirts round . . . I'll give you an example.
This is one, there are loads of others. We had a visitor
from the States, and we'd taken him out, we'd taken
him to the South Bank, no what it was, sorry, we had
collected this guy from Heathrow, and it was this time
last year, actually, it was Good Friday, and this guy had
arrived from San Francisco and was completely jet-
lagged, but what had happened was that Gemma had
gotten us tickets for the 'Matthew Passion' at the
Festival Hall and didn't want to miss it, if you knew her
you'd understand because it's like a very important
thing, annual event to go there and she sits with the
score and is completely . . . music gives her something
which I certainly could never, I look at her sometimes
when she's listening to music and I'm frightened, I feel
lonely, I'm frightened because it's a lover's face, and I
never really see it . . . would you mind if I just opened
the window a little? I think it's the iron, the steam, am
I speaking too fast for you? sorry, I'm sure I'm
completely incoherent . . .

Concepcion (*heavy accent*)   No, no . . . you were at a
concert with an American friend . . . it's okay, I'll do
the window.

Rob   Well, of course, you'll know about jet-lag and

this guy he was very game and sort of sat there propped
up, but I don't know if you know the 'Matthew
Passion', it's not short, it is in fact the opposite of short,
it is fantastically long. I mean it goes on and on you get
an interval of about two hours, it's a marathon, okay?
but of course wonderful, even I see that. Gem's always
saying it has more good tunes in that one piece than in
the rest of, it's great, and she's there following every
bar in her book while this poor American guy is sitting
bolt upright and then every now and then swaying and
then catching himself and going back to upright, then
lurching, then swaying, then bolt upright in this terrible
torture of staying awake . . .

Concepcion Uhuh.

Rob . . . and then we get to the interval and go off to
find some food, because I also realise this guy must be
famished, Alistair won't mind if I take a cup of tea, will
he?

Concepcion Sure.

Rob He's eaten me out of house and home many a
time, so I'm sure he won't . . . I think I'll pinch a
banana, it's ripe anyway, so, mmm, actually I'll just
have juice, I'm not supposed to be drinking tea, is there
any herb? No look: juice is fine, great, so anyway, where
was I? This is really nice of you, you know.

Concepcion It's no problem.

Rob (*flirting a little*) I'd really like to, I really
appreciate it, I do. (*Tails off.*) Where were we? Oh yes,
so we toddle off to find something to eat, and it's now
the middle of the afternoon and our American friend is
sleep-walking and we get to some patio or other, with
all kinds of things going on, do you know the South
Bank? by the NFT and the National Theatre, well
there's always stuff going on, clowns and those funny
dancers and stalls and stuff and buskers and this is all
great for Felix, the American, who, – 'cause there he is

first time in London and he can see the Thames and all
the monuments – and we queue up for ages and get
sandwiches and sit out in the sunshine having, eating,
and getting some fresh air before plunging back into the
Passion, which of course is now getting very heavy and
moving and stuff, so like it's a very welcome break and
Felix is reviving a little with the food and there's
buskers playing, a really nice flautist. I can see it so
vividly, this guy comes round with a cap to collect for
this flautist, who's really wonderful, beautiful sound and
you know what it's like sometimes when you're in the
fresh air and there's music playing it's really lovely and
with a glass of wine and so of course I dug into my
pocket and gave a pound or something, some money for
this flautist who's probably a student at the Royal
College, I think it's standard practice for them to go out
and busk and stuff, so . . . I give him some money and
then we carry on eating and I'm not alone in this there
are loads of people there from the concert, too, all
eating and being entertained and they all give
generously and . . . anyway the point is about ten
minutes later, maybe five minutes, or even sooner, I
can't quite remember, anyway I don't know if you know
that area but it's a real haven for dossers, you know:
down and outs, there are lots of people down by
Waterloo Station, homeless, who can't get
accommodation, it's really awful of course, you drive by
at night and there are these huge fires, particularly in
the winter, there are a lot of people there, there are a lot
of homeless people . . . I'm sure you know all about
this, and what happens of course is that one of these
people, a woman, who had a drink problem, I mean she
was carrying a bottle of cider and she had on a duffle
coat and she smelt and, of course – it wasn't her fault,
but you can't help those people by giving them a pound
coin, you know, because they go and buy a bottle of
cider and get pissed and it's not helping, so I didn't
respond to this woman, and obviously, it was awkward
for Felix, because she kept kind of pestering him, he

looked, you know how all Americans look wealthy, they
sort of exude dollars, and I was quite firm, I suppose,
and anyway, this woman went off, in fact I did give her
50p, as it happens, but it was just to get rid of her, I
really feel strongly that it wasn't helping her in the
slightest, it was just another dousing of the liver, I gave
her 50p and in fact she looked disgusted, she looked so
disgusted I wished I'd just ignored her . . . so . . . and
Gem is watching all this and saying nothing and we
finish our food and we go back to the concert, of course
as I'm telling you this the symbolism is all absolutely
transparent but at the time, as we wander back to the
concert I'm thinking about Felix, who is going a kind of
pale grey at the prospect of another two hours of Bach:
you know I find it quite a strain to sit through however
wonderful but we go back in and all the singers stand
up and of course it's riveting in a way – no, it's
wonderful, – and Felix does fall asleep and then it
finishes and we're on our way back to the car, – great
banana thanks, I was just a little peckish – and Gemma
starts wandering around this area looking as if she's lost
something, which would not be unusual, and so I stand
there holding Felix up, Felix has by this time given up
pretending to be with us, he is in rapid eye movement
dreaming of futons and California and sanity and
Gemma is hunting around the back of the benches and
– sort of urgent and anxious and uncommunicative –
and then she walked down a side road by the Cut, near
the station and sure enough, by one of these huge open
fires, the clusters of tramps, getting near the violent
hour, the windscreen smashing hour, the abuse hour,
Gemma wanders among these people poking around in
their sacks and their sleeping bags and their cardboard
boxes and yes there is our lady from the interval,
settling down with her cider in a black dustbin liner
filled with newspaper, essentially we'd walked into
somebody's bedroom, I tried to make this point later,
unsuccessfully, and Gem bends down and starts talking
to her, 'What's your name? Where do you live?' I'm not

joking. 'Where do you live?' and she said, of course, 'I
live here.' Her name was Muriel. 'I'm Gemma,' says
Gemma 'and this is Rob and this is our friend Felix.
Are you hungry, Muriel?' Muriel was hungry. 'Let me
give you some money. Muriel, I'm going to give you
ten pounds, okay, and I want you to go and buy
yourself a meal.' And out comes this ten pound note.
Ten pounds to the Muriels of this world is not a note,
it is a pale hot liquid in a big bottle. It is half an hour
of a delicious burning sensation. It is not a meal. So I
say this, I am, of course, embarrassed and
uncomfortable and I am propping up Felix who would
not turn a hair before slipping in beside Muriel in the
black plastic bag. Actually what I am is furious, I am
choking with anger. 'Okay', says Gemma, who has gone
that kind of, you know what it feels like to write with a
pencil just after you've sharpened it, like that, like that
is how she went, she yanked Muriel out of the sack and
then we were wandering along the South Bank, because
Gemma was going to find Muriel a place where she
could have a meal, which we would supervise. Felix
hasn't spoken for about seven hours, he's disappeared
into his jacket, he's asleep in his pocket, Gemma walks
purposefully staring ahead dragging Muriel, who is
leaning on me, stinking to high heaven, like a hung
rabbit, like a jugged hare, I can still smell that . . . ach!
anyway, and Muriel is saying 'I'm thirsty, I'm a bit
thirsty, where are we?' and she pulls out her little bottle
of liquor from one of her many carrier bags which have
devolved into my safe keeping and is about to swig from
it when down comes Gemma's avenging hand, yanks
this full bottle from Muriel and sends it flying into the
Thames. We listen in silence as it hit the water. Splash.

Restaurants won't serve the homeless, or drunks, it puts
customers off, they see the bags, they smell the jugged
hare and they're suddenly fully booked or closing or
don't speak English. Eventually we are in the car,
driving in to the West End. Gemma has begun speaking

about taking Muriel home and giving her a bath, giving
her some clothes, oh God, listen Concepcion: I admire
her, I love her, she's extraordinary, she really does, she
means what she's saying, and I admire her, you know
but she's also a complete pain in the neck and the car is
like a medieval kitchen and Felix is getting car sick and
Gemma is getting into a rage, we stop at one restaurant
which is empty and has WE ARE OPEN UNTIL
TWO across its lights, the sign, the façade, and
suddenly it's out of food, and Gemma starts yelling and
kicks out at one of the tables and Muriel is crying and
the manager of this place is ringing the police and it's
all very ugly and Felix is sitting in the back seat of the
car, perched with his head in his hands and his stomach
emptying into the pavement and back go Muriel's bags
and Muriel in beside him and I'm driving along with
Gemma consoling Muriel who is crying and Felix
groaning and I can feel this violence uncoiling inside me
and then Muriel says 'I want to come and live with
you.' and again we all listen in silence as this hits the
water. Splash.

We drove to the nearest Mcdonalds, bought her a Big
Mac with everything on it and left her there eating it.
She was about three miles from where she lived and it
was after midnight. She had beautiful eyes. I suppose
she was fifty, she could have been any age, I suppose
she could have been forty or fifty or sixty, but she had
these beautiful grey eyes and they rested on you as you
spoke. And hoped. With such longing. Whenever I've
witnessed atrocities on television, people starving,
tortured, degraded, abandoned, they've always had
Muriel's eyes, and the same look: Disappointed. I can't
think of a better way of describing the look. Just
disappointed. Disappointed.

Gemma's *flat. Evening.*

The 'Matthew Passion'.

Lorna   It's like uh . . . this is like therapy, isn't it? . . .
I hate analysis, I hate, I hate, I hate the idea of
undressing myself, you know, like making love with a
stranger, worse, worse than that, actually.

We went, Stephen and I, we both went, we went
together, that was to a counsellor and then we went to
see different people, separately, in fact.

I was very humiliated, I was, it was very humiliating
for me, so I, well I've told you, Gemma, about the
sunbed, going for my sunbed, in fact I've got my own
sunbed, which I hide, I've got my own sunbed, which I
do in the evening, and the appointments at the sunbed
were, in fact, appointments with my woman, with this
woman, and I think it was the same for Stephen,
although I think men are able to gloss their day more
easily, aren't they? . . . A screw, the shrink, a drink, can
all fit under meeting. I had a meeting, there was a
meeting, it was a meeting.

No, so there was no sunbed appointment, there was a
therapist, and then of course, as I frantically got brown
in the middle of the night I realised the half-hour under
the lamp was better than anything that was going on in
that terrible room in Swiss Cottage with the blasted
alarm clock and the venetian blind and the joss stick or
whatever it was, and the voice she had, the voice, it was
like, what was it like? It was a sort of whisper, like
you'd talk to a person who was dying, a sort of whisper
for the very sick and I used to boil, honestly, I felt
violence towards her for this voice, and I felt violence
for the silence.

I used to cry, sometimes I would go in and I would cry
for forty-five minutes, and, really, the whole forty-five
minutes, and she would sit and make sympathetic
noises, sympathetic clucks, you know, while I cried, and

then the alarm clock would ring and it would be
finished, but you'd be very good, Gem, because you
have the eyes,
you have the eyes,
do you just sit here all day? what are you doing with
yourself? are you reading? what? writing? I thought of
writing to you. I thought it would be quieter. I had this
theory perhaps the silence was connected with noise, I
know you're sensitive to noise, and music, I love this
(*The music.*) . . . is it, what is it, is it Bach? So I
thought it might just be that you wanted some peace.
When my mother died I went to Greece and just lay in
the sun for two weeks and let the sun anaesthetise me,
let it just, I just lay on the sand for two weeks and let
the sun press on top of me

this is before I had the sunbed

can I smoke? I won't if, thanks, Oh God, I gave you
this ashtray, didn't I? This is the Greek experience
ashtray, isn't that funny? This is from the lying in the
sand holiday, ha! It's beautiful, isn't it?
So I can thank my mother for something, can't I? Paid
for that holiday and the car and the ashtray.

I made a list, that was one of the therapy things, my
therapist didn't ask me to do it, but I did it during that
period, I made a list of all the things I got as a result of
my mother dying, what I did with the money;
holiday
car
I had my hair streaked,
I opened an account, a sort of indulgence account
So I had my hair streaked, and a manicure, and a facial
and I brought some silk underwear and what else? well
I used most of it for the house, I paid for the bathroom,
our bathroom, which means that every time I take a
shower, I say thank you, Mum, whenever I brush my
teeth, whenever I take a pee, thank you, Mum, and the
sunbed of course,

in fact
this is our biggest bond, Stephen and I, what has kept
us at least legally as one,
the fact that we both come from suicide families.
isn't that interesting?
we were married before we found that out,

it wasn't until my mother killed herself that
I discovered his mother had too.
it was like he suddenly came out with it,
snap,
and both so cruel, really, very cruel, very cruel
his mother, he found her, his father had been dead for
some, and he went round, or went home, I think he was
still a student, I don't know all the details, anyway he
found her and she had a note pinned to her dress, and it
said, 'Stephen, put the rubbish out'.
that was all,
'Stephen, put the rubbish out'.

which was very
harsh,
I think . . .

my woman called suicide an act of homicide on the
living

look at that cat!
the two of you
big cat, little cat.
purring, curled up,
it's quite unnerving, ha!
she'll never sit on my lap, will she?
I've got an incapacity to love, Gemma,
that's the
that's the
I think that's the

my ma was wearing one of my dresses
did you know that?
when she killed herself

at least she didn't leave a note
it was a summer dress and it didn't fit

it's very hard to think your way out of
something like that
to be honest
at least she finally managed to do it
she was the Sylvia Plath of South Hampstead,
my ma,
one year in ten
that's where the limp came from
known as the riding accident limp
known as the falling off the horse limp
was in fact the
throwing herself from the high building limp

she, this was when I was eleven,
she booked a room in a five-storey hotel
that was her joke when she told this nasty
little tale
I booked into a five-story hotel in
Eastbourne,
and she
do you know I think that was the most heart-
breaking thing to think that she would have been the
most beautiful woman, her face was so, I can remember
before this happened, or I think I can, but she was so
twisted and, her spine was, well you know that sort of
hunch and she had to teach herself to walk again, and
what was so pathetic which is a feature of our lives, of
our deaths, isn't it? of our gestures, our grand gestures,
is that they are so human, and so trite.
She couldn't find a clear space to jump from,
she got this top room
with a balcony, but the angle or something,
there were balconies and ledges and she had to do some
sort of impossible clamber to get into a position where
she could hit the ground and then she couldn't do it,
she said she hung by her hands for
I don't know, she said an hour

and then she let go

I think she was just tired,
and of course she hit everything on the way down
apparently she didn't lost consciousness and this chap
came to her, he was one of the kitchen staff, she fell
outside the kitchens, that was her favourite part of the
story
I don't know why
this chap came rushing up
and he asked her her name
and she told him a lie
she'd just jumped from this building, she'd
broken her back, her legs, her arms, her
skull, and she told him a lie
she said her name was Angela Carpenter
which was the name of the girl she'd sat next to at
school.

anyway the next time she managed it
– another week and they would have converted the
cooker to North Sea Gas and that would
have been another fiasco –
I'm not sleeping with Rob any more, Gemma
We haven't for a long time, really,
I'm not sure how you found out, but I wish you hadn't
It makes something which wasn't important
become important
with me
you know, it's a thing I do
it rates with not having bra straps on my tan

this is not what I wanted to say
I wanted to say sorry
and say don't worry,

well, I wanted to say sorry

what are you thinking?
Gemma?

what are you thinking?
do you want me to go?

to tell you the absolute truth, for the past
ten minutes I've wanted to slap your face

Gemma's *flat. The Garden. Morning. No music.*

Gemma   When you stop speaking, it's like stopping
eating. The first day there's something thrilling, and
new, before the pain begins. The pain where you want
to give up, where you can think of nothing else.

Then the second day, you feel wretched, the third
delirious, and then suddenly there's no appetite, it
shrinks, it shrinks, until the prospect of speaking, the
thought of words retching from the mouth, how ugly
and gross it seems.

Nothing changes.

How to stop people in their tracks, and make them
think. Only if you're starving, if it's your son lying in
your arms, or you think he might be in that discarded
pile of mutilated bodies, or there's no milk in your
breast and the baby's crying, or the radiation is leaking
into your child's lungs, or the lead or the nitrates or
the, or the, or the and all the while skirts get longer,
skirts get shorter, skirts get longer, skirts get shorter,
poetry is written, the news is read, I buy a different
butter at the store and have my hair permed,
straightened, coloured, cut, lengthened, all the while my
hair keeps growing, I throw away all my skirts, a black
bag to Oxfam, lately I've been at Oxfam buying back
my skirts, I've stripped the pine and painted the pine,
pulled out the fireplaces and put them back in, I'm on
the pill, I'm off the pill, I'm on the pill, I'm off the pill.
I'm listening to jazz, swing, jazz, swing, I'm getting my
posters framed. I'm telling my women's group
everything. I'm protesting. I'm protesting. I've covered

my wall with postcards, with posters, with postcards, with posters. No this. Out them. In these. Yes those. No this. Out them. In these. Yes those. The rows. The rows with my friends, my lovers. What were they about? What did they change? The fact is, the facts are, nothing is changed. Nothing has been done. There is neither rhyme nor reason, just tears, tears, people's pain, people's rage, their aggression. And silence. ⟩

Look, already it's happening here, the weight of words, the torrent, all the words being said seep into each other, the rage, the protest all clotting together, sit and listen to the wireless and run the wheel of the tuner, spin the dial, hear them all at it, in all languages, pouring out. This is, after all, our first punishment – Babel – saying so much to say nothing. Doing so much to do nothing. Because the power to arrest, to stop us short in our tracks, what does that?

Pause.

but the silence, listen, how rich it is, how pregnant, how full . . .

Pause.

What do you remember? When all is said and done? A kiss? The taste of someone's lips? A view? A breath? A tune? The weight of your grandmother's coffin? The veins on your mother's legs. The white lines on her stomach.

Don't speak for a day and then start looking. The senses are sharp. Look at the world about its business. The snarl. The roar. Skin stretched over the teeth. The madness.

The law is frightened of silence. It has words for the defendant who becomes mute. The wrath of God. Mute by malice. But it's not silence which is the punishment. Words. WORDS are the punishment.

The silence.

A silence.

beautiful
last year it was cigarettes,
the year before chocolate
but this is the best

*The Aria. 'Mache dich, Mein Hertze, Rein' from Bach's
'St Matthew Passion'. Magnificent. Released.*

Hang Up

for Jonathan Lunn

Hang Up was first performed as a dance duet at the Sadler's Wells Theatre and first broadcast on BBC Radio 3 in November 1987. The dancers and the voices were as follows:

	Sadler's Wells		Radio 3
	Voices	*Dancers*	*Voices*
He	David Threlfall	Jonathan Lunn	Anton Lesser
She	Juliet Stevenson	Lauren Potter	Juliet Stevenson

Choreographed by Jonathan Lunn

Radio broadcast directed by Robert Cooper

The bedroom in his house.

A telephone rings. It's answered. **He** *is in the room.* **She** *is distant. We hear music at her end. Occasionally we hear Telecom line noises.*

He   Hello.

She   It's me.

He   Hello.

Pause.

She   It was getting late so I thought I'd call.

He   Great.

Pause.

She   Is it a bad time?

He   No. (*Pause.*) No, no. It's a. How are you? No, it's a good time.

She   Good. I'm fine. I'm tired. I'm fine. I'm tired. Are you, what are you doing? You weren't asleep?

He   No. I wasn't asleep. I'm not asleep. I was, I wasn't doing anything. I'm fine. I'm great. I was just here. What are you listening to?

She   What?

He   The music.

She   I don't know. It's the radio.

He   Right. Sounds good.

She   It's too loud, I'll turn it down.

He   No, it's fine, I can hear you, it's nice, it gives me a sense of what, where you are, the room, the . . .

She   You know where I am, I don't mean you, I mean me, I can't hear you properly, (*The music decreases in volume.*) that's better.

He   It's odd, because I don't think of you as listening to music.

She   Well, I do.

He   Yeah.

She   It's because we don't have the same taste.

He   What does that mean?

She   What I said, you don't think of me listening to music because we have different tastes, so when I've been with you, I haven't particularly wanted to listen to anything, or you know, then I feel you'll ask me what I'm listening to, or why I've tuned the radio to a particular station or, anyway, let's not have a big inquest into what music we listen to.

He   Have you got somebody with you or something?

She   No, I haven't. And that's cheap isn't it, actually, to ask that.

He   Is it? Why?

She   You know why, because it just says you don't trust me, when I'm away you don't trust me, and that's not a good feeling, it makes me feel I constantly have to defend everything I'm doing when I'm not with you, so when you ask me what sort of day I've had you're actually asking me whether I've been faithful to you. Which is not a good feeling, so that I feel you're asking me what I'm listening to in case it's a clue or something, you know: Christ!

He   Don't be ridiculous. I was asking you what music you were listening to because I could hear some music on and I wondered what it was and because – I just said – I miss you and you're not with me and I was trying to visualise where you were, what you were doing, what you looked like, and the room, and what you were listening to, it's got nothing to do with clues . . .

She   Except you say is there anyone in the room with

me, and I feel you're creating this thing, because you can be really paranoid, honestly, and I can just see you thinking: you see! She's in the room with somebody and she's listening to music and everything and before I know it I'm having an affair. So please. Just. You know.

He I'm sorry. Okay. I'm sorry. Christ, I hate this, I hate not being able to, everything becomes out of, I mean, Christ, I'm just asking about a piece of music, I wish I'd never bothered now, because . . . (*sighing*.)

She Right. Listen, are you going to call me back? Because if we're going to talk more, you'd better call me, because it's not my house and –

He Right.

She What?

He Right, I'll call you back.

She If you'd rather not . . .

He Of course I want to call you back, come on!

She Okay.

He I'll put the phone down.

She Right.

He I'm putting it down. 'Bye.

Phone down. Rapid fade out.

Fade up on her hallway – we hear the same music coming from another room. Phone rings and is picked up immediately by her. **She** *is in hallway.* **He** *is now distant.*

She Hello.

He It's me.

She So . . .

He This is a better line.

She Yes.

He I'm missing you.

She   Thank you.

He   Don't say thank you. Say you're missing me.

She   I'm missing you.

He   Are you?

She   I'm going to have to borrow a fire tonight, I think, or something, because it's so cold in this room – the radiator's supposed to be on, but it's freezing – so yes, I'm missing not being at home. Yes. Okay?

He   Which home? My home? Your home?

She   Both. They're both warmer than this place.

He   Okay.

She   My bed at home doesn't have you in it, so your bed would be best.

He   My electric blanket.

She   And your electric blanket.

He   And my radiators.

She   And your radiators. *My* hot-water bottle.

He   *My* carpet in the bathroom.

She   Your carpet in the bathroom.

He   I'm missing you.

She   Did you go out tonight, or what?

He   No. I hadn't called, because, no I did go out briefly, I was out earlier for a while, but I was going to call you late because I wanted to have this conversation last thing, you know: go to sleep with your voice still uh. What's the bed like?

She   Okay. It's okay. It's not great. It sags a bit. It sags a bit. It's okay.

He   Were you planning on coming back at the weekend, or what?

She I don't know yet. I don't know. I'll see. Maybe. Why?

He No, it's just that if you weren't, if you can't, maybe I could come over, if that's a good idea, I'll come over there and you know: sag in your bed.

She Okay. Obviously, if I have to work on Saturday, it wouldn't be, I don't think there'd be much point, would there? it would be a long way to come for one day, but if I'm not, I've got a feeling we will though, because that's always the way, isn't it?

He Right. Sure.

She The one weekend you'd like off.

He That's right.

She What's your week like?

He Fine. Fine. You know. Fine. I don't know. Yes.

She Have you seen anybody?

He No. Not really. I've seen a few people. At work, obviously. I've had lunch and things. But not, no, not really, no, just pottered about.

She So what was it this evening?

He What?

She Where were you when I was waiting for you to call me?

He Were you waiting for me to call you? I was going to call you at eleven, I was just thinking that and then the telephone rang.

She No, well I was going to go to bed and I thought I'll get into bed and then the phone will ring, because it's out in the hall and otherwise I'm standing in a t-shirt in the hall and it's really public, me and the bicycles and the hall and – in fact – I wear your dufflecoat. I'm using it as a dressing-gown. I wear your dufflecoat to the loo. So I thought I'd ring before all that, because otherwise people come back and there I am.

He   That's nice. I like the thought of you wearing my dufflecoat. No, I saw my friend, Susie.

She   What?

He   This evening, I saw my friend, Susie. We had a drink. It wasn't arranged. I bumped into her, so we had a drink, a quick drink.

She   Why do you do that? Say that? 'My friend' like that? You don't have to say that.

He   What do you mean?

She   You know what I mean, calling her *my friend* as if that, as if by saying that it doesn't count or something, because you can just say you had a drink with Susie and that's fine.

He   Okay, I had a drink with Susie.

She   Fine.

He   Who's my friend, you know.

She   No, you wouldn't say, I was having a drink with my friend David, would you:

He   I might, I might, I don't know, and anyway I don't live with a man, if I lived with a man I might feel the need to distinguish between friends and anything else, not that I live with you, but you get the gist, I don't know, this was what I was saying earlier to my non-friend, friend, Susie as it happens, that a lot of this has got to do with not actually doing it, not actually being able to make a commitment, because everything then gets so complicated because obviously you need to look at your place and then you're away, or I'm away and there just aren't enough days or normality, of just simple days without, there's nothing simple, I can't remember what I was going to say now, what was I saying? To do with having both flats. I can't think, well

it just means nothing feels firm, so I don't relax and
then I end up sounding like I'm worried there's
someone in the room with you, which I am – I suppose,
in my heart of hearts, I do – and so much time just
spent talking without seeing you and not laughing, not
doing things together and . . . this is not what I was
trying to say, I had a really clear sense of it when I was
talking, earlier, it's hopeless, and I'm still wondering,
whether you're alone. I wanted to go over to your flat
and ransack it, I didn't want to, but sometimes, I get
very wound up and then I want to go over and just
ransack and place from top to bottom.

She   Have you? I hope you're joking, because if –

He (*interrupting*)   I said, I haven't but sometimes –

She (*interrupting*)   I promise you, if I thought you'd
gone over to the flat when I wasn't there, I couldn't
forgive you, Christ, I feel so stifled sometimes.

He   I said, I haven't been over to your flat. I said I
sometimes get the urge to. I haven't been to your flat. I
haven't been anywhere near it.

She   Anyway. I feel very tense about that. I feel very
strongly about it. I think you should give me back the
key.

He   Okay. I didn't ask you for the key. You gave me
the key so I could check the mail and the answerphone,
but I'm very happy to give you the key back.

She   And I'm aware of what you're trying to say, what
you were saying earlier, about things being complicated,
they are, but that's a choice we've made, isn't it? And
we both agreed and like everything sometimes it works
and sometimes it doesn't, but it means we're not
possessions, we're not taking each other for granted,
we're not the carpet in the bathroom.

He   Sometimes I'd like to be the carpet in the
bathroom.

She Sometimes you are. Sometimes I am.

He Yeah. I know. I know. Do you know, this morning on the tube, I got an early tube and it was, it wasn't crowded or anything, and the lights didn't work properly, they kept fading out, and we kept stopping for signals, but anyway, the point is opposite me, on the other seats, there was this couple and they were both, they were thing, mildly sub, handicapped, obviously not severe, they looked ordinary enough, but they were reading comics, children's comics and . . . the *Beezer*, you know . . . *Bunty* . . . and, anyway, as it started stopping and the lights are coming on and off every five minutes and I realised what they're doing, they're starting to giggle, and what's happening is, every time the lights go off they're kissing, just kissing and then springing apart as the lights come on, so the lights would go off, then come on, and there'd be this flurry of activity and then they'd spring apart and read their comics with these huge grins, because they'd been kissing, and I just thought, Oh God, I miss you and I love you and where are you? So, I guess, well I'm sad today, that's all. It was so tender. And I just . . . (*Sighs.*) Are you still there?

She Yes.

He I don't know what I'm talking about.

She There is someone here.

He Right.

She I didn't see the point in telling you. There seemed no point. It's just hurtful.

He Right.

She Because it's nothing. You see, Christ (*sighs.*) it's nothing. It's nothing, for either of us, for him either, but now it's something. And I didn't mean it to be. It's nothing.

He So you rang me so I wouldn't disturb you.

She   I can't say anything. Whatever I say now. How can I say anything?

He   I knew anyway.

She   What? What did you know?

He   I knew you were with somebody.

She   How?

He   I went to your flat.

She   I don't believe you.

He   That's why I saw Susie. I had to speak to somebody. I went to the flat and then I called Susie. I had to tell somebody. So. I told Susie.

She   Is Susie there now?

He   No.

She sighs.

He   I should go.

She (*suddenly loud*)   Please, would you turn that off. (*Pause.*) I'm talking to you.

The music is turned off.

Thank you.

He   What?

She   I was asking for the radio to be turned off, I can't think, I can't cope with the music. I wasn't talking to you.

He   I'm going.

She   I'm sitting on a bicycle.

He   What?

She   I'm sitting on a bicycle. Someone's bike in the hall. Listen. (*A cycle bell rings.*) That's the bell. I could just peddle off in my t-shirt and dufflecoat.

He   In my dufflecoat.

She   Yeah.

He   Peddle down to me.

She   Shall?

He   Yeah, please.

Pause.

She   It's very quiet now. Which phone are you on?
Upstairs?

He   Yes.

Pause.

She   Don't hang up.

Pause.

I've only ever known one mentally handicapped person.
This was years ago. He was my age, and sweet, really
very sweet, and he had a girlfriend and she was deaf
and dumb. Nobody could understand her, honestly,
nobody, she wouldn't sign or anything, the sign
language: she wouldn't, but this guy doted on her, he
had the kind of personality would be patient with
anybody. He'd push an old person around in a
wheelchair all day if they wanted, real patience, and
with children, and he was the same with this deaf and
dumb girl and the way he understood her, the way they
got on together was he talked for them both, so like
he'd ask her a question and then do the answer for her:
'Want a cup of tea?' 'Yes please.' 'Do you want sugar?'
'Yes please, two please.' 'Cup of tea, two sugars,
coming up,' and that's how they got on together, it was
perfect. (*Back to the present.*) It's nothing. I would have
told you, probably. I don't know. I wouldn't have told
you. There's nothing to tell. I'd like to cycle down to
you now. Darling?

Pause.

Darling? Are you still there?

He *sighs.*

'Yes, I'm still here.' 'Good, I thought you'd gone for a minute.' 'No, still here.' 'Good, because I wanted to tell you I'm missing you too.' 'Thank you.' 'And we'll be all right, I'll cycle down to you, in my t-shirt and my dufflecoat, all night and we'll be fine.' (*The cycle bell rings again.*)

He puts down the receiver.

Johnny? Johnny? (*Beat.*) Johnny?

Silence.

What If It's Raining?

*for Hannah and all those
to whom we ran for cover*

'If I loved you, they said, I'd leave
and find my own affairs.
Well, once again this April, we've
come round to the bears;

punished and cared for, behind bars,
the coons on bread and water
stretch thin black fingers after ours.
And you are still my daughter.'

Heart's Needle, W.D.Snodgrass

What If It's Raining? was a Limehouse production, first shown on Channel 4 in 1986, with the following cast:

Dominic	Michael Maloney
Marilyn	Deborah Findlay
Philip	Miles Anderson
Jack	Jack Bentall
Joseph	Bernard Paddon
Siobhan	Eve Matheson
Chris	Chris Jury
Angie	Kamilla Blanche
Stephanie	Jane Gurnett

Director Stephen Whittaker
Producer Mark Shivas

Part One

Dominic/Marilyn's *house. Thursday. Early evening.*

Dominic *is in his study. His son* **Jack** *in one arm, drawing with the other. He is a cartoonist. He draws on huge pieces of paper. The one he's working on now has the sheet divided into four boxes.*

1. A baby crying in a father's arms.
2. Father trying to amuse the baby.
3. Father frantic to amuse the baby. Toys, noises, funny faces.
The baby bawls.
4. Father asleep. Baby bawls.

Dominic *adds the caption: 'Getting Baby off to Sleep'. The cartoon completed, he turns his attention to* **Jack**. **Jack** *has been patiently sucking on anything within reach, but he needs getting off to sleep himself.*

Dominic (*to* **Jack**) Where's Mum, eh?

Mum – **Marilyn** *– is late.* **Dominic** *wants to go to a launch party for a book he has illustrated, but he cannot go until she gets back. He puts lids on pens, stands and carries* **Jack** *through to his bedroom. He lays the baby in his cot.* **Jack** *is quiet.* **Dominic** *stands by the door for a second, then dims the light and makes to go.* **Jack** *cries.*

Dominic (*coming straight back in*) Not going to go to sleep, eh?

He picks up the baby and they go downstairs to the kitchen/dining room. **Dominic** *puts* **Jack** *in his high chair, and quickly prepares him a bowl of cereal. The television is on, flickering. A string quartet bleeds through from the stereo.*

Dominic Now listen, rat face, scoff this muck, okay, and get tired! And I won't listen to any more excuses.

Asleep in five minutes or bum severely bitten. (**Jack** *cries.*) Hey, I was joking. I'm sorry darling.

Philip's *flat. The same time.*

Philip *owns a shop which sells paintings, antiques and beautiful things. Upstairs is his flat. This is equally tasteful; indeed many of the things here are part of the population which is for sale.*

Marilyn *is here, wearing only a shirt. She begins getting herself together to leave.*

Marilyn   I'm so late.

Philip   You could say the exhibition held you up. You wanted to discuss rehanging stuff or whatever.

Marilyn   I mean for the baby.

Philip   He'll be asleep.

Marilyn   No. Well, maybe.

Philip   How is Dominic with him? He dotes on him, doesn't he?

Marilyn   He dotes on his photographs. He's fine with him. Yes.

Philip   But?

Marilyn   I feel as if I've spent the entire evening criticising him. (*Pause.*) He undoes everything I do. I don't think he means to.

Philip   What are you doing? (**Marilyn** *is scrabbling around by the couch. She finds her knickers and holds them up to him.*) Oh right.

Marilyn (*dressing*)   I do love him. That's the point. And I come here to see you, to talk, to be myself a bit, and . . . (*She's trying to excuse the affair.*)

Philip   What?

Marilyn Making love. It's getting to be a habit. How did it start?

Philip When you go to see people, to talk, do you always take your diaphragm with you?

Marilyn That's not fair, Philip.

Philip Well let's start off being honest, shall we? And see how long it lasts.

Dominic/Marilyn's *bedroom. A little later.*

Dominic *is dressing for a smart function. Clothes on the bed, everywhere. He's late. He pauses as he hears*
Marilyn *coming in, the doors quietly thudding as first she checks downstairs, taking in the mess, the television droning, the lights left on, then comes upstairs to check on* **Jack.** *She comes into their bedroom.*

Marilyn Sorry. When did he go off?

Dominic Early. Then he woke up.

Marilyn Why?

Dominic I've no idea.

Marilyn How come all the rooms downstairs have everything turned on?

Dominic What everything?

Marilyn The TV. Everything.

Dominic I'm actually very late.

Marilyn I know. I said sorry. The gallery, the exhibition, there were things to sort out.

Dominic Right. How's Philip?

Marilyn He's fine. You know.

Dominic *(putting on his shoes)* Look, I owe him a pound. Will you give it to him? And I think Jack's getting more teeth or something. His bottom's sore again.

Marilyn   Did you change him before he went off?

Dominic   Yes.

Marilyn   You have to put loads of that cream on because he wets himself and it gets rinsed off . . .

Dominic (*interrupting her*)   I know. I did that.

Marilyn *realises she is being over-anxious. A pause.*

Dominic   Look, uh, I'm probably going to get landed with bringing some of the people back. It's the form. So bear with me, eh? It'll be late. We'll probably have to eat first. (*Pause.*) And I'm not sure where Joseph's going to stay the night.

Marilyn   Why do you have to say it like that? Probably this, probably that. You know full well you will eat, and they will come back, and Joseph will stay here. Why not just say that?

Dominic   Because that's how you respond. Why don't you come? I'm sure Pippa would uh . . .

Marilyn   Why ask now?

Dominic   It's the first book I've illustrated. It's important to me. I don't want to have to ask you. Anyway I'll see you Marilyn.

He is about to leave, but **Marilyn** *speaks.* **Dominic** *stands framed by the door.*

Marilyn   Is it just tonight?

Dominic   No. Tonight's the university thing. Tomorrow night's the publishers. I told you.

Marilyn   You didn't, actually. And it's not in the diary. (*Pause. Softening.*) Good luck.

Dominic   Thanks.

Marilyn (*gently*) And I hope nobody likes the book and you get dysentery from the curry.

Dominic Lasagne.

Marilyn I'll try to come tomorrow, okay?

Dominic *nods. He exits.* **Marilyn** *surveys the wreckage of the bedroom.*

Dominic/Marilyn's *house. A few hours later.*

Marilyn *opens the front door to* **Philip**.

Philip Bad time?

Marilyn *is surprised. Before she can answer,* **Philip** *assumes 'yes'.*

Philip Right.

Marilyn (*stopping him before he leaves*) Good time. Come in.

Philip *comes in. He is wearing a cap.*

Philip I came disguised. How did you recognise me?

Marilyn (*flustered*) Do you want a drink or something?

Philip Hey, I'm not staying, don't panic. I was just passing.

Marilyn Where are you going?

Philip Home.

Marilyn Where've you come from?

Philip Home. This is directly on my way back. I have a voucher which says you owe me one kiss. (*He produces a small piece of paper.*) Is this your signature?

In spite of herself, she laughs. She gives him a polite kiss, then pulls his cap down over his eyes.

I missed you.

Marilyn   I've only been gone a few hours.

Philip   I've been missing you a few hours.

Marilyn   Safe journey.

She opens the door and gently pushes him out.

Dominic/Marilyn's *house. The same day. Late.*

The front door opens and **Dominic, Joseph** *and* **Siobhan** *come in unloading coats, high-spirited.* **Joseph** *is small, bespectacled. Rather serious, rather feeble. He wrote the book which* **Dominic** *has illustrated.* **Siobhan** *is a postgraduate and President of the University Literary Society. She has organised the evening.*

Dominic   Sssh! Keep it down because Jack's asleep.

They go into the kitchen. **Dominic** *turns on the light.*

I'll just report in. Then I'll pop the kettle on. No, I'll pop the kettle on then I'll report in. Or would you rather have a scotch Joseph? Siobhan? Tea? Coffee?

Siobhan   I'll have the scotch, if that's okay?

Dominic   Yes, of course it's okay. (*Changes his mind again.*) Listen I'll just say hello upstairs. Then I'll sort you out.

Joseph   Thank you.

Dominic (*exiting*)   Excuse me.

Siobhan (*to* **Joseph**, *smiling*)   I'll put the kettle on.

Dominic/Marilyn's *bedroom. Dark.*

Dominic (*at the door*)   Darling?

Marilyn *is asleep. He moves to the bed, switches on the table lamp, and nuzzles up to her.*

Dominic   Darling?

Marilyn Ngh?

Dominic Sorry it's so late. You okay?

Marilyn Ngh.

Dominic Listen, I've said it's all right if we put Joseph up.

Marilyn Uh-huh.

Dominic Did Jack wake up? Oh and some people have come back for a coffee.

Marilyn Did you have to wake me up to tell me these things?

Dominic I just wanted to check about Joseph.

Marilyn What if I'd said no?

Dominic I think it was a success.

Marilyn What was?

Dominic This evening.

Marilyn Uh-huh.

Dominic And we did have curry. And Joseph's threatening dysentery. (*He laughs into the duvet.*)

Marilyn Right.

Dominic Right, well I'll see you in a sec, then. I'll just run Siobhan home and come back to bed.

Marilyn Why can't she get a cab?

Dominic It's all right. I won't wake you. And if the baby does, I'll see to him.

Marilyn (*disbelieving*) Yeah.

Dominic (*kissing her*) Night, night, cynic. You smell nice.

Marilyn You smell of tandoori.

Dominic (*correcting her*) Sag Gosht.

Marilyn Same to you.

Dominic *exits. He's left the light on.* **Marilyn** *leans over to turn it off.*

Dominic *driving* **Siobhan** *home.*

VW Beetle pops along the streets. **Siobhan** *is very keen on* **Dominic.**

Siobhan   I like the book, Dominic. Very much.

Dominic   Thanks.

Siobhan   Fantastic drawings. Beautiful.

Dominic   Oh, I think the text is the thing. Joseph's extraordinary.

They arrive.

Siobhan   Thanks for driving me home. I could easily have walked.

Dominic   No trouble. Um, how's your research?

Siobhan   Oh, slow. Lot of time asking myself why I'm doing it. A lot of time doing other things. Like tonight.

Dominic   Hey, yes, thanks for tonight. I'm sorry I'm not better at it. When two or three people are gathered together I'm a disaster.

Siobhan (*genuinely*)   I don't think so. By the way, I'm happy to baby-sit tomorrow. I mean not only for your squash, but the whole evening if Marilyn would like to go to the do with you.

Dominic   Thanks very much. I might take you up on that. She's got an exhibition for Oxfam. But um . . . Anyway.

Siobhan   The way you and Marilyn live restores my faith in the institution. Because you lead your own lives, give each other space.

Dominic You lower your expectations. That's how things work. I sometimes think that's what maturity is. Lowering your expectations.

Siobhan Have you ever been attracted to anyone else?

Dominic (*a little manipulative*) Uh, have I ever been attracted to anyone else? Well you see I mean, the clever thing about marriage and kids and things is that it sort of guarantees you're just too busy surviving really, to do anything about it. Even if you were.

Siobhan (*feeling in her pockets*) I hope I've got my key . . . Yes.

Dominic Thanks for . . .

Siobhan Thank you.

They embrace briefly. A polite kiss.

Dominic (*as she gets out*) You all right there?

Siobhan Yes.

Dominic Sleep tight.

He relaxes back into his seat, turns on the car stereo, pleased with himself, then drives off.

Dominic/Marilyn's *bedroom. A little later.*

Dominic *is fast asleep.* **Marilyn** *enters, carrying a wide-awake* **Jack**. *She gets into bed, putting baby between herself and* **Dominic**. *She whispers to* **Jack***: sleep would be in order.* **Jack** *is not persuaded. He begins to wail.* **Dominic** *is fast asleep.*

Dominic/Marilyn's *house. Kitchen/dining room. The following morning.*

Marilyn *enters, late: she has to take* **Jack** *to* **Hilary**'s. *She is well-dressed despite the rush.* **Joseph** *is at the* *fridge, visibly embarrassed at being found holding a carton of milk.* **Marilyn** *has probably only met* **Joseph** *once or twice before. She moves quickly around the kitchen, preparing a lightning breakfast. She has* **Jack** *under one arm as she does so. She's very capable.*

Joseph   Ah. Hello. I'm just making –

Marilyn   Go ahead.

Joseph   Is it all right if I use this milk?

Marilyn   Help yourself.

Joseph   Dominic did tell –

Marilyn   You're welcome to stay. I'm sorry, I'm late. I'm sure when Dominic gets down he'll tell you where everything is . . .

Joseph   Oh, I don't need, I can . . . as long as I'm not.

Marilyn *isn't paying a great deal of attention.* **Joseph** *retreats to cereal and a book.* **Marilyn** *puts* **Jack** *in his chair and ties a pink bib round his neck.*

Marilyn   Incidentally, this is the brat. Jack, this is Joseph.

Joseph   It's a he, yes?

Marilyn   It is. (*Deadpan.*) Hence the pink.

Joseph   I'm afraid I don't know much about children.

Marilyn   Nor do I.

Joseph (*disbelieving*)   Oh . . .

Marilyn   No, really. By the way, I love the book. It's marvellous.

Joseph   Thank you. That's the nearest I've got to childbirth.

Marilyn   What is?

Joseph   Writing the book. I felt as though I were giving birth.

Marilyn (*unimpressed*)   Why was that?

She does not require a reply, but **Joseph** *offers one nonetheless. It is lost, because* **Marilyn** *is talking to* **Jack.**

Marilyn   Now look, are you going to eat something instant or do we have to hang around for boiled egg? Egg, huh? Okay, I'll join you.

As **Marilyn** *busies herself with the eggs,* **Dominic** *enters.*

Dominic   Hey, why didn't you wake me?

Marilyn (*genuine*)   You were tired. You were asleep. (*She hands him a mug of tea.*)

Dominic   Thank you. Morning Joseph. How did you sleep?

Joseph   Well. Fine.

Dominic *ignores him as* **Marilyn** *did; he goes to* **Jack.**

Dominic (*cooing to* **Jack**)   Hello! (*To* **Marilyn.**) Darling. I'll take Jack to Hilary's. You'll be late.

Marilyn   No, I need the car. I'm going back to the exhibition.

Joseph   What's this?

Marilyn   It's an exhibition I'm organising for a local gallery, for Oxfam. It's by Chilean refugees. It's mostly wall-hangings. You should come and see.

Dominic   If you see Philip remind him we're playing squash at six o'clock.

Marilyn   You're playing squash with Philip?

Dominic   I told you. And that girl – thing, the Literary Society girl . . . Siobhan. She said she'd sit for us the whole evening. If you do want to come with me to the jamboree.

Marilyn   I don't know. I'm not playing squash, anyway. Liz is away.

Dominic   Well come and play with Philip and me. We can swap round.

Marilyn   I don't know. (*To* **Jack**.) Are you going to have blackcurrant?

Dominic   I'll feed him, darling, and you can get ready.

Marilyn   Or I can feed me.

Dominic   Or I could feed you and he could get ready. (*They laugh.* **Dominic** *looks to* **Jack**. *Puts on his cooing voice*.) Hey! He slept through! No wonder we're all so jolly! (*To* **Joseph**.) Sorry about this, Joseph: blissful family life.

Squash Court. The same day, 7pm.

A squash ball slams into the wall. **Dominic** *is playing* **Philip**. **Dominic** *is having to do more of the running.*

Through the glass back wall of the court, **Marilyn** *watches* **Dominic** *lose the game. She is dressed for squash herself.* **Dominic** *loses, huffs, puffs. Then he turns and speaks through the glass to* **Marilyn**.

Dominic   Come in and rescue me.

Marilyn   No, you carry on.

Dominic   No, no, no: I've lulled him into a false sense of security. You'll demolish him now. (*He comes heaving out of the court*.) 'Specially in those shorts.

Marilyn   Shut up.

Dominic (*holding the door for her to go in*)   Take my advice. Cheat. (*Kisses her*.) I'll go and ring Siobhan and see if Jack's okay.

Marilyn   Great.

Dominic   Philip, cheers. Thanks very much.

Dominic *exits.*

Philip Play for service?

He hits the ball onto the wall. They play silently.
Marilyn *misses. She picks up the ball, serves, begins to cry. They play for a few seconds.* **Marilyn** *sinks to the floor and sobs.*

Marilyn God, Philip. What are we doing? What am I doing? What am I playing at?

Philip *kneels and comforts her.*

Philip Come on, let's play.

Marilyn I can't.

Philip What are you doing after this?

Marilyn There's a promotional thing for Dominic and Joseph's book. I'm supposed to be going.

Philip Spend the evening with me.

Marilyn I can't.

They get up.

Philip I'll take you home.

Marilyn We've got a sitter.

Philip I'll take her home. Then I'll come back.

Marilyn Philip, I can't.

Philip You can do anything you want. If you don't want to, don't.

Dominic *appears at the court door.*

Dominic Who's winning?

Philip Oh it's uh . . . pretty even.

Dominic Well hurry up and finish. I want to –

Marilyn Dom, I'm feeling a bit sick. (*Aside to* **Philip**.) I do actually feel as if I could throw up.

Dominic (*coming into the court, concerned*) Hey, are you okay?

Marilyn Yeah.

Dominic Well look, you've probably overdone it a bit. Let's get you sat down.

Marilyn I think I'll get changed.

Dominic Okay.

Marilyn Philip said he'll take me home.

Philip No problem.

Dominic (*deflated*) Oh . . . it's just that –

Marilyn I know. Your promotion thing. It's just that I feel a bit sick.

Dominic Look, if you're worried about the baby, Siobhan said he's fast asleep.

Marilyn It's not the baby. I just don't feel up to –

Philip It really is no problem to take her home.

A beat. **Dominic** *is not happy.*

Dominic Right.

Marilyn/Dominic's *bedroom. Later that evening.*

Marilyn *and* **Philip** *are naked on the bed. Intent, holding each other.* **Marilyn** *suddenly disengages.*

Marilyn (*explaining*) Jack.

Now we hear a sob.

Philip What?

Marilyn He's woken up. Sorry. (*Quickly gets out of bed and grabs her dressing-gown.*)

Philip Do you always go straight to him?

Marilyn Yes.

Philip Doesn't he ever go back to sleep by himself?

Marilyn No.

Marilyn *goes through to* **Jack**'s *bedroom. She picks him up and starts trying to pat him off to sleep.* **Philip** *comes in, dressing himself at the same time. He comes up behind* **Marilyn** *and puts his arm around her and the baby.*

Philip I love you. I'd love you both.

Marilyn If we ever came to you, he'd break all your beautiful things.

Jack *miraculously settles down.* **Philip** *and* **Marilyn** *smile. The world full of sign and portent.*

Dominic/Marilyn's *bedroom. Later.*

Marilyn *is asleep in bed.* **Dominic** *gets in.*

Dominic Hi. You feel nice.

Marilyn (*hazily*) What time is it?

Dominic Dunno.

Marilyn Have you been drinking?

Dominic Yeah. (*He moves up against her in the bed.*)

Marilyn Dom, I really need to sleep.

Dominic Then why did you put your cap in?

Marilyn (*waking up fast*) What?

Dominic I am a private detective. I snooped in your bathroom, and could not find the object in question. I submit, madam. Have your evil way with me.

Marilyn Are you doing this deliberately, Dominic?

Dominic Doing what?

Marilyn Because if you are, it's sick, that's all.

Dominic (*deflated*)   What's sick? That I want to make love with you?

Marilyn   Oh Christ. (*She sits up.*) I think we should talk.

Dominic   I don't want to talk. I'm drunk. I want to make love with you.

Marilyn   Great.

Dominic   Well it may not be great, Marilyn, but it's what I feel.

Marilyn   And I feel we should talk or sleep.

Dominic   Yeah. Okay.

Abruptly, he rolls over to go to sleep. Long pause.

I'm trying to count sheep. And they've all got erections.

Busy Park. The following afternoon.

Marilyn *and* **Philip** *are walking, pushing a sleeping* **Jack**.

Marilyn   Do you need to get back?

Philip   Probably.

Marilyn   Thanks for coming with us.

Philip   Will Dom be at home?

Marilyn   Yes. He's working. He's got a cartoon to finish and it's late.

Philip   I'm glad.

Marilyn   Why's that?

Philip   Otherwise I couldn't have seen you.

Marilyn   Oh, we never do this, Philip. That's not how we work. Our day is inched out into schedules and permutations: Dom/Jack, Marilyn/Jack, Dom work/

Marilyn work. Dom out/Marilyn in, Marilyn out/Dom in. And so on. And so forth.

Philip   Why?

Marilyn   Why? Well because of who we are. What we want. Because of him. And because of me. (*Pause.*) Anyway I'm going to have to say something about us.

Dominic/Marilyn's *house: kitchen/dining room. The same day. Late afternoon.*

Marilyn *comes in to find* **Joseph** *at the table, eating and reading: feed the brain. Elsewhere on the table there is evidence of shopping in quantity: wine, pasta.*

Marilyn   Hi.

Joseph   Hello.

Marilyn   What's all this?

Joseph (*guilty*)   Oh. I was just feeling a bit peckish. Hope you don't –

Marilyn   No. I mean the shopping.

Joseph   Dominic got it for tonight.

Marilyn   For what tonight?

Joseph   Well, at the thing last night, he invited Christopher and the chap from Penguin – well, anyway, it's four, I think. Plus you and Dominic.

Marilyn   Right.

Marilyn *goes to the table in the hall and checks the diary. She goes upstairs to tackle* **Dominic**.

Dominic *is in his study, working on his cartoon strip. This one shows a sleepless man in bed counting sheep. The sheep have erections.* **Marilyn** *comes in.* **Dominic** *doesn't look round, but continues drawing. His stereo is playing. As they talk he rejects ideas and screws up quantities of paper.*

Dominic (*of the mess*) I know, sorry. It's a tip.

Marilyn Why do you do this? (*The cartoon, the sheep.*) It used to be funny. It's not funny any more.

Dominic Oh, I never find it funny.

Marilyn You do this instead of talking.

Dominic No, I do it instead of fucking, actually. Speaking of the second to last time we did that, where's Jack?

Marilyn He's downstairs. He's asleep in the hall. I wanted to talk tonight. I didn't want to have people round here for dinner.

Dominic You're very keen on this talk all of a sudden. (*He is still drawing frantically.*)

Marilyn Will you look at me?

He slowly takes off his glasses, switches off the music with his remote control, then turns at last to face her.

Dominic I'm not joking when I say I have to finish this. I have to get it round to them this evening. I'm sorry. It's my work. It's not Oxfam. It's not deserving. It probably is a complete confection, but it's what I do and I get paid for it. Inviting publishers round is part of the business. (*He puts his glasses back on and starts working again.*)

Marilyn I'm very unhappy, Dominic.

Dominic Well right. That's why you want to talk. You've yet to come in here and say 'I'm happy: I want to talk.'

Marilyn Are you happy with me being like this?

Dominic I love you.

Marilyn Dominic, darling. That's not what I asked. Anyway, what's the point? When I do say anything it only ends up in one of your pictures.

Dominic (*drawing frantically*)   I'm trying to remember the last time you called me darling.

Marilyn (*angry, frustrated*)   Dominic, please. (*She turns to leave.*)

Dominic   The Chinese, on the other hand – did you know this? – the Chinese have no word for darling –

Dominic *is cut off by the sound of the door slamming behind* **Marilyn**. *He looks round at the closed door, then clicks on the music and returns to work.*

Dominic/Marilyn's *house: downstairs. That evening.*

Marilyn *is sat at the table. It is laid for the dinner party. There is pasta on the stove.* **Marilyn** *simmers along with the sauce.* **Dominic** *bounces in through the front door.*

Dominic (*calling*)   Darling! (*Comes into the kitchen/ dining area. Sees the food. Sees* **Marilyn**.) Hi. Smells good.

Marilyn   I thought you said you'd be back at 7.30.

Dominic   Oh, Alan was there and some people it was important to meet. What should I do? (*He means the food.*)

Marilyn   It's done.

Dominic   Oh. (*Excited.*) Hey, it went really well. Oh, and I've got a thing in *Harpers*! Good, eh?

Marilyn   Tremendous. Dominic –

Dominic (*not listening*)   Where's Jack? Is he asleep?

Marilyn   I think so. Dominic –

Dominic (*not listening*)   Thanks for doing this, darling. (*He means the food, which he stirs and tastes.*) Must have taken you ages. Did you use a stock cube?

Marilyn I'm going up to my parents' tonight.
(**Dominic** *turns, concerned.*)

Dominic Why? What? Is somebody ill? What,
Marilyn?

Marilyn I need some time on my own. To think.

Dominic Oh, what, is the baby getting on top of you?
(*Decides that's what it is.*) Yeah, me too. I know.
(*Planning.*) All right. I'll drive you up first thing in the
morning. Actually – no I can't, uh –

Marilyn I want to take the baby with me. And Philip
said he'd drive us.

Dominic Why Philip?

Marilyn Because I think I'm in love with him.
(*Pause.*) I've been trying to tell you.

A long pause. **Dominic** *stirs the sauce, not looking at her.*

Dominic This 'love'. (*He makes the word sound
unpleasant.*) It's a mutual love, is it?

Marilyn Yes.

Dominic (*still stirring*) You screwing him, are you?
(**Marilyn** *does not reply.*) In our bed?

Marilyn Dominic . . . don't.

Dominic I want to know if you've been fucking in
our bed?

Marilyn Yes, we have.

Dominic Right. How many times? (*No reply.*) What
are you pausing for? You counting?

Marilyn Don't do this, Dominic. Please.

Dominic Philip? Oh Christ. (*Pause. Turns to her,
sudden realisation.*) Of course! your cap!

The doorbell rings. **Marilyn** *gets up quickly.*

Marilyn   That'll be Philip. He thought he ought to come round, so we could talk.

Pause.

Dominic   Oh yeah. Let's have Phil in for a chat.

Marilyn   Shall I go? If you don't want to see him. I'll ask him to wait in the car. (*The bell rings again.*) Well?

Dominic   Let Philip in, Marilyn.

Marilyn *goes out to the hall. Sound of voices. She reappears with* **Joseph**.

Marilyn   It's Joseph.

Dominic   Hello Joseph. Silly: we thought you were Marilyn's lover. (**Joseph** *is dumbfounded. He grins inanely. The doorbell rings again.*) Oh no – that'll be him now. I'll go.

Dominic *opens the front door. It is* **Philip**.

Philip   Dominic.

Philip *walks past him towards* **Marilyn** *and* **Joseph**, *who stand motionless at the other end of the hall.* **Dominic** *closes the door and puts his back to it, silently watching* **Philip** *and* **Marilyn**.

Marilyn   I think we'd better just go, Philip.

Philip   Okay.

Marilyn   Will you apologise to the others for me, Joseph? I have to go up to my parents' tonight.

Joseph (*pathetic*)   Of course.

Marilyn   See you again, I hope. (*She moves to the door,* **Philip** *following.*) I'll be back on Sunday, Dominic. But I'll give you a ring tomorrow night.

Dominic *says nothing. He just looks at them, his back to the door.* **Marilyn** *and* **Philip** *move upstairs to get the baby and his things.* **Dominic** *at last leaves the door and goes through to the kitchen/dining room, passing a* *fantastically uncomfortable* **Joseph** *in the process. He sits down at the table.*

Joseph   I'm in the way, I know. Can I do anything? I think I should just go and get changed.

Joseph *shuffles out awkwardly.* **Dominic** *sits. The sound of the front door closing behind* **Marilyn**, **Philip** *and* **Jack**.

Siobhan's *student house. The middle of the night.*

Dominic *and* **Siobhan** *enter the kitchen, having agreed on coffee.* **Siobhan** *is wearing her dressing gown.* **Dominic** *a leather jacket.*

Siobhan   It's instant.

Dominic   Thank you.

Siobhan   Can I ask why you are not at home?

Dominic (*the question does not register*)   I don't suppose you could manage something to eat, could you?

Siobhan   Uh –

Dominic (*suddenly realising that this is asking a lot*)   No, actually, no. Coffee'll be fine.

There is a long pause. **Dominic** *stands by the door, as if unwilling to commit himself to staying.* **Siobhan** *is busy with the kettle and the coffee.*

Siobhan   Does Marilyn know you're here?

Dominic   No. No, she doesn't.

Siobhan   I see. (*Not seeing at all.*)

Dominic   Could I stay? I mean, the spare bed if you like.

Pause. **Siobhan** *turns, smiles nervously.*

Siobhan   There isn't a spare bed.

Dominic   The floor, then.

Siobhan   You can sleep in my bed. I'll have the floor. I can sleep anywhere and you look bushed.

Dominic   Why don't I just borrow your dressing gown and promise to behave? (*Suddenly unsure; he doesn't know what he is doing.*) No, thank you, I must go –

Siobhan (*she stops him going*)   No, please. It's no problem. Why don't you use the bathroom, and I'll bring the coffee to bed?

Siobhan *could do with some reassurance that this is the best plan, but* **Dominic** *shuffles out – obedient rather than keen – to the bathroom.*

Siobhan's *bedroom. A few minutes later.*

Siobhan *is sitting up in bed, still wearing the dressing gown. The hall light is on. A shadow arrives, and knocks.*

Siobhan   Come in.

Dominic *comes in. He's wearing only T-shirt and knickers. He carries his clothes in front of himself like a shield.*

Dominic   I haven't brushed my teeth.

Siobhan   What?

Dominic   I can't go to sleep without brushing my teeth.

Siobhan   Well you can use my toothbrush.

Dominic   Oh Christ. I'm trying to remember the last time I got into bed with someone else.

Siobhan   Is Marilyn away? (*No reply.*) Will you not tell me why you've just suddenly turned up?

Dominic   Dunno.

Siobhan   Well, can I say I'm happy you did?

Dominic   Thanks.

He sits on the edge of the bed. Doesn't know what to do next. **Siobhan** *hands him the coffee.*

Siobhan   Your coffee.

Dominic   Oh, right.

Siobhan   And you wanted to borrow my dressing gown?

Dominic   Yes please.

Dominic *sips his coffee and puts the mug down onto the floor. As he is doing this,* **Siobhan** *is removing her dressing gown. When he looks at her again he sees she is naked. He is thrown.*

Dominic   Oh.

Siobhan   I'm not on the pill, Dominic. That's the only thing.

Dominic   Uh. Uh. I have to go now.

Siobhan   Why? Because of that? Because I'm not on the pill?

Dominic   No. No. Not because of you. Nu uh – (*Covered in confusion.*) Marilyn's left me, Siobhan.

Siobhan   What do you mean, left you? For good?

Dominic   Maybe. Well, for the weekend. (*Thinks.*) Maybe. I don't know.

Long pause. Neither moves.

Siobhan (*struggling for a little dignity*)   Well, there's no reason why you can't sleep here anyway, is there?

Dominic   You're really lovely. Do you know that? (*Pause.* **Siobhan** *does not respond. She's hurt.*) Look, I'll call you tomorrow, okay? (*He tries pecking her on the forehead. No response.*) It's just that I'm supposed to have been at a dinner party. And it was *my* dinner party. So I'd better get back and do the washing up. I'll

call you tomorr – oh I'm sorry. I'm all over the place
tonight. (*Still nothing. He picks up his clothes to leave.*)
Sleep tight, eh?

He leaves.

Bristol, **Philip**'*s new shop. Saturday morning.*

Philip, Marilyn *and* **Jack** *explore a property in a
trendy part of the city. It's part of an old arcade which is
being redeveloped and restored. Lovely. Like* **Philip**'*s
other shop, this one has living space above.*

Philip   Well. What do you think?

Marilyn (*she looks*)   It's okay. It'll be nice.

Philip   Good, I'm glad. Because I want you to come
and live here with me.

Marilyn *is shocked. She looks at him.* **Jack** *in her arms,
she moves away, through the shop, up to the flat. She
surveys the bare rooms.*

Philip (*picking up the conversation again*)   I bought this
place for us to live in.

Marilyn   I don't believe you.

Philip   It's true.

Marilyn   That's the most absurd thing I've ever
heard.

Philip   Maybe. (*Calm, logical.*) I wanted to open up
another shop. I wanted to live somewhere else. I wanted
a life with you. This place came on the market.

Marilyn (*unimpressed*)   And now I have? Well, that
was useful. (*Pause.*) I don't think I'm ready to live with
you.

Philip   Why not?

Marilyn   What about Dominic? What about my job?

Philip (*reasonable*)   I want you to come and live here with me. If you want to.

Marilyn   He needs changing. (*She means* **Jack**.) I'm sorry. Can we go back to the hotel? He'll sleep. Then we can talk. (*They move to go back.*)

Philip   We could sleep.

Marilyn   I'm not tired.

Philip   We could go to bed anyway.

Marilyn   And I'm worried about solving everything in bed.

Philip   Why?

Marilyn   Because – I don't know. Look Philip . . . Just give me some time. I want to feel . . . (*Doesn't know what she wants to feel.*)

Philip   It's okay.

Marilyn   Is it? Is it okay? (*She doesn't think it is.*)

Philip   I didn't mean –

Marilyn (*continuing*)   Because it feels terrible. It feels to me that nothing, that how can anything good come from hurt, from beginning in hurt? and I feel guilty about saying I was going to my parents and then coming here. And not calling . . . I don't know. It doesn't feel okay.

Philip   If I thought there was a marriage to break up. If I thought I was destroying something then I wouldn't –

Marilyn   Well how could you? If there was a marriage I wouldn't have let you. (*Continuous thought.*) You see, how could Dom see Jack?

Philip   It's not that far. It took us two hours to drive here. I want you to know I'll take care of you. And Jack. I promise.

Marilyn Philip, that's not the point.

Philip (*simultaneously*) Wait till you see how well I change nappies.

Marilyn Oh, I can imagine, Philip.

Philip There's nothing here. (*The flat.*) Whatever we did, we could do together. Starting from scratch.

Marilyn (*loving him*) Philip.

Philip What?

Bristol. Hotel room. Sunday morning.

Marilyn, *in her nightshirt, brings* **Jack** *into the bed. Her side, not* **Philip's**; *he is apparently sleeping.*

Philip (*sleepily*) Hello.

Marilyn I hope you don't mind company.

Philip No.

Marilyn This is a bit of a tradition.

Philip I like it.

Marilyn Do you? Do you mind if he comes in the middle? (*Explaining.*) Then he doesn't fall out.

Philip No. Of course I don't mind.

Marilyn *puts* **Jack** *in the middle.* **Jack** *gurgles and plays with a toy.*

Marilyn (*apologetically*) Passion-killer.

Philip You think so? (*Wraps his feet round hers.*)

Marilyn Do you like him? (**Philip** *smiles.*) Shut up, Marilyn.

Philip Yes, I like him. (*Pause.*) And I like you. And I like this dimple, and this mouth. And this nose. (*He touches dimple, mouth, nose.*)

Marilyn (*cheerful*)   Not these eyes, huh?

Philip (*as if making a tough decision*)   I quite like the eyes.

Marilyn   I've got ugly hands. (*Shows them.*)

Philip (*holds them*)   They're not ugly. They're beautiful.

Marilyn   No they're not.

Philip   Okay then, I like your ugly hands.

Marilyn (*sternly*)   Good. You'd better. Because I can't change them.

Philip   And I like here. (*Touching under the quilt.*) And here. (*He puts his hand to her breast.*)

Marilyn (*laughing*)   Get off!

Philip   I mention no names in front of the infant.

Marilyn   I'm glad.

Philip   Hm?

Marilyn   Thanks for this time. It's been good.

Philip   It has. It has been good. Can I hold one of your ugly hands? (*They hold hands.*) The thing is, Marilyn, you can stay with Dominic, and feel righteous, and nobody will blame you, and you'll maybe survive. Or you can come to me, and everybody will blame you, and it will involve all kinds of pain, but if you do come, it will be because you want to come, and it will be honest. And Dominic will gain – I think – because he will be forced to consider what he really wants, and not just drift along, which he does. He plays at being married, and that's not good enough for you.

Marilyn   But he loves me, Philip. And he thinks it's good enough for him.

Philip   How does he know?

Marilyn   How do you?

Philip I can feel you. I can feel how much of your heart is going spare.

Marilyn (*loving him*) Can you?

Philip Yes.

They kiss. **Jack** *gurgles.*

Outside **Dominic/Marilyn**'s *house. Monday morning.*

From his study window, **Dominic** *watches* **Marilyn,** **Philip** *and* **Jack** *arrive in* **Philip**'s *car.* **Marilyn** *and* **Philip** *unload.*

Philip Good luck. Do you want me to come in with you?

Marilyn No. I'll call you.

Marilyn *turns with no gesture of affection, and enters the house.* **Philip** *looks up suddenly at* **Dominic**'s *study window. An impulsive wave as he meets* **Dominic**'s *stare.* **Dominic** *reciprocates, equally impulsive – then catches himself in mid-wave. A beat.* **Philip** *gets into the car and drives off.*

Marilyn *goes into the kitchen/dining area.* **Dominic** *has cleaned up: everything is spotless, immaculate. A vase of flowers on the table. She puts* **Jack** *in his chair and sets about making him some food.* **Dominic** *comes in and goes straight to* **Jack**.

Dominic Hello, fish face! How have you been? (*Pretends to listen to* **Jack**'s *reply.*) Did you? Oh, have you? Well, I didn't have such a good time. I went down the swings. Played hide-and-seek, blind man's buff: usual sort of weekend. (*Excited.*) Oh! I did some drawing and colouring in!

Marilyn Dominic. (*He has ignored her so far.*)

Dominic (*lightly*) Hi. Good weekend?

Marilyn   I don't think good or bad comes into it.

Dominic   Really? How odd. What does come into it?

Marilyn (*ignoring this*)   Were you all right? Did you manage? I intended to come back last night, but . . .

Dominic (*not listening; notices that* **Jack** *is wearing new dungarees*)   Are these new?

Marilyn   Yes. They're lovely, aren't they?

Dominic (*to* **Jack**).   Oh, they're pretty sexy. (*Looking at him, admiring.*) Do you think he looks like me today?

Marilyn   Everybody says so. Will you have some coffee?

Dominic   How are your folks?

Marilyn   I didn't see them.

Dominic   Oh?

Marilyn   You knew that.

Dominic (*in mock confusion*)   No, sorry. I thought you'd said you were going down to your parents for a few days. To think.

Marilyn   Dominic. I spoke to my mother last night. She told me you'd spoken to her.

Dominic   Right.

Marilyn   So why did you ask me how she was?

Dominic (*ignoring the question*)   Oh, incidentally, one thing that can be said for heartbreak: it's great copy.

Marilyn   Please, Dom

Dominic   No really, it's true. (*He is speaking as if he is still telling* **Jack** *about his weekend.*) Last night, of course, I expected you back. So while I kept vigil; the drawings! Well, I couldn't stop. And some of them are very funny, though I say so myself. (**Jack** *cries.*) Oh all right, then: quite funny.

Marilyn   I have to go to work.

Dominic   Right, back to the gallery.

Marilyn   No.

Dominic   I must say, on reflection, I was pretty dim, wasn't I? When Philip suggested hanging that exhibition in his gallery, I thought, that was terribly philanthropic. I thought (*enjoying this alliteration.*) how philanthropic of Philip. There you go.

Marilyn (*persevering*)   Thanks for making everything so tidy. It's beautiful. And the flowers.

Dominic   Right.

Marilyn   Why did you have to wait until now to do it?

Dominic (**Marilyn** *had made* **Jack**'*s food*)   Can I feed him?

Marilyn   Of course.

Dominic (*to* **Jack**, *cooing*)   'Cause I missed him. I missed you, brat face. There was nothing to do all night except sleep.

Marilyn   Listen, I won't go to work this morning. I'll ring the office. We could take him out for a walk. How does that sound?

Dominic   Okay.

Marilyn   Okay. I'll go and call. I really think we need to talk. (**Dominic** *does not look at her. Continues feeding* **Jack**.) Dom? (*No response. She gives up.*) I'll go and call.

Approach to a children's playground. The same morning.

Dominic *and* **Marilyn** *are pushing* **Jack** *towards the playground. It is cold. They are less tense.*

Dominic   So where did you go? Or do you not want to discuss that? I don't mind.

Marilyn   It's okay. Bristol.

Dominic   What, a hotel?

Marilyn   Yes.

Dominic   Mr and Mrs Philip?

Marilyn   Shut up.

Dominic   Did you have to take Jack with you?

Marilyn   Come on Dominic. He's never spent a night apart from me. Apart from anything else it's pretty obvious we have a dependency on each other. I've hardly stopped feeding him.

Dominic   What's the difference between your being responsible to Jack and being responsible to me?

They reach the park. They nod at a mum they both know.

Marilyn   Look, are we really going to talk? In which case, let's go home and talk.

Dominic (*loud, embarrassing*)   I don't want you to leave me. Can I make that clear? Am I making that clear? I don't want you to leave me.

Marilyn   Dominic.

Dominic   And I don't want you in somebody else's bed. And I particularly don't want my son in someone else's bed. (*Pause. Thinks.*) Oh God, I've just thought of that. Did he go in the bed with you? Christ.

Marilyn   No.

Dominic   Christ.

Marilyn *is holding* **Jack** *in her arms. She sits on the roundabout. Pushes it a little.*

Marilyn   Philip is going to move to Bristol. He wants us to move with him.

Dominic Does he.

Marilyn You're telling me what you want. I'm telling you what he wants.

Dominic Why should what he wants figure in our marriage? In our family?

Marilyn Let's go back, Dom. It's not fair to do this out here.

Dominic Fair? Is it fair you're not giving us a chance?

Marilyn I've given us *years*.

Dominic (*desperate*) I love you. I need you.

Marilyn (*suddenly*) Do you want me to say I won't see Philip?

Dominic What?

Marilyn I could try not seeing him.

Dominic What's the point? What's the point if you don't want to?

Marilyn I don't know. Let's go back, eh?

Dominic (*sullen*) No, I think I'll stay here. I'll see you later.

Marilyn Oh Dominic. Okay.

Dominic Will you leave the baby? (*She opens her mouth to express doubts, but he anticipates.*) I haven't been with him. I want to be. Just for a few minutes. I'll bring him back.

Marilyn They said it was going to rain, Dom. I don't want him to get wet.

Dominic (*slowly*) Yes, well, if it rains we'll come back straight away.

She gives **Dominic** *the baby. He holds him tight. Sits on the roundabout.* **Marilyn** *hesitates, then turns and walks away.* **Dominic** *and* **Jack** *spin slowly on the roundabout.*

Part Two

Outside **Dominic/Marilyn**'s *house. Early evening. Some weeks later.*

Dominic *drives up in the Beetle and gets out.* **Marilyn** *greets him at the car. She's holding the baby. She has her coat on, ready to go out:* **Dominic** *has agreed to baby-sit for her.*

Marilyn (*warmly*) Hello.

Dominic (*business-like*) What time will you be back? (*Hands* **Marilyn** *the car keys.*) It needs petrol.

Marilyn (*concerned*) Are you okay, Dom?

Dominic (*business-like*) Tremendous. (*He takes* **Jack** *from her.*) We'll see you later.

Dominic *carries* **Jack** *into the house.* **Marilyn** *sighs and gets into the car.*

Philip's *flat. Early evening.*

Marilyn *and* **Philip** *are in the process of packing up* **Philip**'s *belongings for the move to Bristol. His things are being divided up into those which will be sold in the new shop, and those which will be kept as ornaments or whatever.*

Philip *is considering a beautiful African figure. It is an old man carved in wood, three feet tall, smiling benignly.*

Marilyn (*horrified*) You can't sell him!

Philip I think we'll need the space.

Marilyn Why?

Philip Your stuff. The baby's. It's not that big a space.

Marilyn There won't be that much. I don't want to take any of the things from the house.

Philip I see. (*He hadn't realised this.*)

Marilyn Well, obviously things that are mine, were mine before. But nothing else.

Philip Okay.

Marilyn Because he's losing me and Jack. It's not fair he should lose anything else.

Philip Hey, why are you telling me all this? Marilyn, it's you I want, not your fridge-freezer.

They hug.

Marilyn Sometimes I wish I could rub everything out and start again with us.

Philip And the baby.

Marilyn And the baby.

Philip Dominic?

She disengages.

Marilyn I don't know. Maybe I don't wish that.

Philip Is work all right? Are they going to give you a watch? (*As a leaving present.*)

Marilyn Probably. (*Pause.*) Gossip is rampant. For a charitable organisation, it doesn't manage much between its staff.

Philip And Dominic? Has he agreed to meet us somewhere?

Marilyn I haven't asked him. I'm sorry. I will. It's just – if I dwell on him I can't move . . . He paralyses me. He's paralysed. I'll get back tonight and he'll go as soon as I walk through the door. He won't talk. Have you read this month's *Harpers*?

Philip   Why? No, should I?

Marilyn   There's a cartoon.

Philip   And?

Marilyn   Well, of course, the thing is, if you didn't know about us it wouldn't mean anything. But it's pretty hurtful.

Philip   Well, it's understandable.

Marilyn   Yes. Just stings a bit, that's all.

Philip   That's all. (*Wry smile.*)

Marilyn   That's all. (*Wry smile.*)

Dominic/Marilyn's *house. The same time.*

Dominic *has an ironing board out.* **Siobhan** *sits at the table, watching him iron his clothes. He's baby-sitting while* **Marilyn** *sees* **Philip**. *She's baby-sitting him. And he needs it. Despite* **Siobhan**'s *efforts,* **Dominic** *remains steadfastly grim-faced.*

Siobhan   I don't understand you ironing clothes and then shoving them into a holdall.

Dominic   I like ironing.

Siobhan   Well, why not iron some of Marilyn's things and do yours when you get back to Chris's?

Dominic   If I iron Marilyn's clothes, she'll think I'm getting at her. She hates ironing.

Siobhan   So do I. It's a historical thing.

Dominic   What is?

Siobhan   Women hating ironing. Centuries of oppression.

Dominic   There haven't been irons for centuries.

Siobhan   Oh yes there have.

Dominic   Yeah. I suppose so. Look, I just like ironing. I find it therapeutic. Okay?

Siobhan   I think you hide behind it. It's like a weapon. Don't come close or you'll get your fingers burned.

Dominic   Maybe.

Siobhan   You want me to go, don't you? Before Marilyn comes back.

Dominic (*not entirely honest*)   No.

Siobhan   Doesn't fit the victim bill to have me around.

Dominic   Hey. Don't. And I don't want to be a victim.

Siobhan   Then why did you move out?

Dominic   Uh –

Siobhan   And why have you done nothing, gone nowhere, for weeks? Told no one what's happened? (*Gently.*) Why won't you sleep with me?

Dominic   I dunno.

Siobhan   You won't sleep with me because it means you'd have nothing over Marilyn. You couldn't feel self-righteous.

Dominic   No. I'm sorry you feel like that. I don't feel that's what I'm doing.

Siobhan   It is what you're doing, Dom. You string me along. I mean, why come and sleep in my bed – because you do *sleep* with me – so why not *touch* me? It makes me feel repellent to you.

Dominic (*weakly*)   You're not. You're beautiful. (*He continues to iron.*)

Siobhan   Iron, iron.

Dominic (*looks at her. Irons. Shrugs*)   Iron, iron.

Siobhan   And it's ridiculous baby-sitting while Marilyn sees Philip. (*Long pause.* **Dominic** *ironing.*) I'm going to the Lake District next week. Why don't you come?

Dominic . No thanks. I've got work to do.

Siobhan   Yes. I saw. (*Bitterly.*) Am I the ageing virgin? (*Referring to the illustration in Harpers.*)

Dominic   Ah! Is that why you're being like this?

Siobhan   Why are you doing that rubbish?

Dominic   Fame and fortune. I get propositioned in the supermarket.

Siobhan   Yes, it *is* why I'm being like this. For the record. I just don't understand why you won't talk, but you do this oblique slagging off of Philip and Marilyn in print. It, it stinks.

Dominic   Yeah.

Siobhan (*sharply*)   And putting yourself down in the process doesn't mitigate that!

Dominic   No.

Siobhan   No!

Dominic   What time is it?

Siobhan (*demolished*)   It's all right. I'm going. (*She gets up very quickly and almost runs to the door.*)

Dominic (*not wanting her to go*)   No. I just –

Siobhan (*coming back in, thawing*)   I'm sorry. I didn't intend to lose my temper. I'm sorry. I know it's . . . well, you know I know. And you can come round if you can't sleep and put your head on my shoulder. And toss and turn all night, and peck me on the cheek and that's fine and I won't tell anyone. (*Pause.*) And iron bloody iron.

She goes. **Dominic** *shrugs. Irons.*

Dominic's *room. Later that evening.*

Dominic *is drawing.* **Marilyn** *appears, cautious.*

Marilyn Hi.

Dominic Hi.

He immediately starts collecting his pens and equipment. Gathers his drawings together, puts them into an art folder.

Marilyn Did he get off all right?

Dominic Yep.

Marilyn And he ate everything?

Dominic Yeah. He was great.

Marilyn Good. Thanks for –

Dominic (*cutting her off*) Right. Okay. I could come over tomorrow if you want to go out.

Marilyn Yes. Thanks. (*Struggling.*) I mean, I don't know if I will but you can come over anyway . . . I mean obviously, you know, whatever.

Dominic I did some ironing.

Marilyn I saw. Thanks.

Dominic I was doing some of my own, so –

Marilyn I said thank you.

Dominic No. No, I just meant . . . Forget it. I'll see you.

Marilyn Am I supposed to feel guilty because you ironed some of my clothes? Because I washed all of your clothes for *years*.

Dominic (*doesn't want to hear*) Okay.

Marilyn I just didn't tell you every day. 'I washed some of your clothes today'. Didn't seem very interesting.

Dominic   Yeah, well I go to the launderette now. It's terrific. I get a service wash. I get clean clothes without the poison in the final rinse. (*He has all his things. Puts on his jacket.*)

Marilyn   Well, that's all right then.

Dominic   Absolutely. So, if you'd ring me at Chris's and let me know whether you'll be out or not tomorrow.

He goes past her to leave. **Marilyn** *grabs him, tugging on his jacket.*

Marilyn   Is this it? Dominic? Is this how we're going to be with each other?

Dominic (*the victim*)   I don't know.

Marilyn (*exasperated*)   Christ, Dominic! Why won't you talk, say something?

Dominic   Like?

Marilyn   Like, what's going on? I do actually care about you, you know. About where you are. How you're coping. If you're sleeping. Your parents . . .

Dominic (*exaggerated sarcasm*)   Oh, we're *fine*. How are you? And your parents?

Marilyn   Oh, Christ!

Dominic   Marilyn, listen. You've ditched me for someone else. It's perfectly clear, isn't it? What's there to discuss? Whether I like it? I don't. Whether I'm happy? I'm not. That's about it, isn't it?

Marilyn (*quietly*)   Yes. But for me to know that, you needed to tell me.

Dominic   Oh right. I've got it. Sorry. Right. Well let's just write this up on the wall, shall we?

He removes a picture from the wall by the door. Takes a thick, indelible felt marker. Scribbles 'DON'T GO!' on the wall.

Okay? Is that clear? Can you read that?

Marilyn (*close to tears*)   I can read it. But I don't believe the things you write. To tell you the truth.

Dominic   What?

Marilyn   I think your cartoon strip in that magazine is cheap. And it hurts me.

Dominic (*not entirely honest*)   It's not about you.

Marilyn (*disbelieving*)   No.

Dominic   No.

Marilyn   No, the desperate virgin.

Dominic   Oh God. Right Marilyn, can I just say one thing here before I piss off again to make way for your lover – whom I assume comes complete with washing machine – and that is, if there's one thing about you which hurts me, it is your infinite capacity to absorb any pain, or admission, or any, or, I mean it just doesn't seem to make any odds: you just *soak* it up. (*Looking her in the face. Quite cruel.*) My sense of you, is of this moving sponge which travels purposefully in a single direction, and will just sort of sponge right over me. Irrespective of what I say or do.

Marilyn (*stung, fighting back the tears*)   I don't feel like a sponge. I care about you. I worry about you. But I don't think I want to live with you. Is staying with you the only way I can show you I care?

Dominic   You want to go, you go. I won't give you permission to leave. I won't drag our marriage around like some cripple. If you don't want me – us – you jigger off.

He picks up his things for a second time, and leaves.
Marilyn *sinks into the couch.*

Chris's *flat. Later that evening.*

Dominic *is slumped in the front room of* **Chris**'s *flat.*
Chris *has been putting* **Dominic** *up for the past few*
weeks. **Chris** *is a long-standing loyal friend. He affects a*
boorish, abrasive, chauvinist manner. While **Dominic**
slumps, **Chris** *scoffs a takeaway Chicken Tikka Masala*
at the coffee table. He's just come back from his evening
class in typing.

Chris   You sure you don't want some of this? It's
good.

Dominic   Positive.

Chris   You got to eat, Dom

Dominic   I have.

Chris   So've I. But I'm so depressed about that typing
class, I had to eat again.

Dominic   Why do you do it if you hate it so much?

Chris   I hate the class. I'm in love with the women.

Dominic   Which women?

Chris   All of them. All of them. There are a dozen
nubiles with magnificent chubbies. All different species
and under twenty. That's why I'm so depressed.
(*Considers the food.*) I can't eat all of this. D'you know
one of them's called Gloria. Can you imagine it? There
are actually girls called Gloria. She smiled at me like I
was her uncle. Then I thought – well, I *could* be her
uncle. She showed me how to set my margins.

Dominic   And why typing anyway?

Chris   Typing's a brain-wave. Only young girls, gay
men and me want to do it. Anyway, I'm giving it up. I
can't do it, and (*sitting back, full.*) I'm getting fat.
(*Pause, nervous.*) How was *your* night?

Dominic   Hopeless.

Chris Right. Look, Dom. When Janet left me, that was it. End. Finish. Full stop. But with you, half the neighbourhood is queuing up as a substitute.

Dominic That's not true.

Chris What about the student: Siobhan?

Dominic One person is not a queue.

Chris And what's-her-name was round here like a flash with the Red Cross parcel, crooning all over you.

Dominic She wasn't. She was just being kind.

Chris (*doubtful*) Yeah.

Dominic Anyway, that's only two.

Chris Christ, it's early days yet. All I got was spaghetti bolognese round at your house and Marilyn being smug.

Dominic She wasn't smug.

Chris She *was* smug. So were you as a matter of fact. You sort of crouched in a concerned way. It really pissed me off.

Dominic Thanks a lot.

Chris Well. I wanted alcohol and help slagging Janet off.

Dominic She's a great woman, and you know it.

Chris Christ! See what I mean? And she's okay. She's not great.

Dominic I'm not going to criticise Marilyn. What's the point?

Chris Or Philip? You'd think he was a saint, listening to you. (*Pause.*) They're trampling all over you, Dominic, and you know it.

Dominic No.

Chris Well yes, actually. Look, you're baby-sitting

while your wife goes out screwing and you don't think you're being trampled on. You move out so that she doesn't get inconvenienced. Come on, Dom. It's a farce.

Dominic   Am I in the way or something?

Chris   Get drunk! Hit somebody! Philip preferably. Or Marilyn. But talk about it. Have a breakdown or something. But let it out for Christ-sakes. It's like living with a shaken up coke can.

Dominic (*shouting*)   Is it?

Chris (*shouting*)   Yes it is!

Dominic (*thawing, almost laughing, shouting*)   Well, I'm sorry.

Chris (*shouting, laughing*)   And I'm sorry. (*Quieter.*) It's a bugger what's happening to you and Jack.

Dominic (*subdued again at the mention of* **Jack**)   Yeah. Anyway. I'm going out.

Chris   Siobhan's place?

Dominic   Dunno. Maybe. (*He dips a chapati into the curry.*)

Chris   Finish it.

Dominic   No. (*But he dips in another piece.*)

Chris   Finish it! Look, Dom. Go round to that beautiful woman, get laid, and be grateful.

Outside **Dominic/Marilyn**'s *house. Later that night.*

Philip's *car is parked outside the house.* **Dominic** *is standing across the street, watching. There's nothing much to watch. He's been there a long time. A neighbour walks by with a dog. A light comes on in the house, upstairs. Silhouette of* **Philip**. *Then* **Marilyn**. *A kiss. Then the light goes off again.* **Dominic** *walks across the street to* **Philip**'s *car. He kicks the door panel as hard as he can.*

*He is immediately embarrassed. Bends down to examine
the dent. He rubs at it. Looks about him furtively. Then
slinks off down the road.*

*Health Food Shop Cafeteria. A Saturday afternoon some
days later.*

Philip *and* **Marilyn** *have been doing some shopping for
the new flat. Bags and treats around the table of salads
and other worthy food.* **Jack** *is in a high-chair, next to*
Philip, *who is feeding him.* **Marilyn** *is restless,
distracted:* **Dominic** *is outside.*

Marilyn   Philip, he's still there, across the street. I'm
going to go out and say something to him.

Philip   I don't think you'll have to. (**Dominic** *is
making his way towards the cafe.*)

Marilyn   Oh, Christ. I sometimes thinks he gets some
kind of kick – (*Trails off and looks down.*)

Philip   Marilyn. (*No response.*) Marilyn. (*He squeezes
her hand. She looks at him.*) It's us. We're okay. It's
okay.

Dominic *arrives at the table.*

Dominic   The market's very good here. What did you
buy, anything nice?

Philip   Will you join us?

Dominic   Why not? (*He sits down.*) I'll sit next to my
son.

Marilyn   Do you want some food?

Dominic   Oh, I don't think so. Looks a bit too pious
for me. (*Looks at their bags.*) A lampshade!

Philip   We're shopping for the flat in Bristol.

Dominic   Yes, I'd guessed.

Pause.

Marilyn Dominic, if you don't want to eat, what do you want? –

Dominic I stood outside for half an hour. I thought you might have found the time to come out and talk to me.

Marilyn I didn't see you.

Philip I did, Dominic. I just didn't know what you were hoping for.

Dominic Good old Philip, eh? Honest to a fault. (*Mock query.*) Is that the expression?

Philip I think there's a facetious response to anything I might say to you, Dominic.

Dominic (*fast, bitter*) You're right. Yes, there is. (*To* **Marilyn**.) So. *We* came to this market to get the things for the baby, remember?

Marilyn Yes.

Dominic And then here. You couldn't eat properly because your bulge kept bashing the table.

Philip (*intervening*) Would you prefer it if we left? We could find somewhere to talk. You could come back to the gallery.

Marilyn It wasn't this cafe. Not that it matters. But for the record. It wasn't this cafe.

Dominic It doesn't really matter which cafe it was, does it?

Marilyn (*speechless*) Well . . .

Dominic No. (*To* **Philip**.) I came to see you. They told me at your gallery I'd find you here.

Philip Right.

Dominic I owe you some money for the damage to

your car. Can I write you a cheque? (*Reaches inside his jacket for the cheque book.*)

Philip It took me five minutes to get the dent out. It didn't cost anything.

Dominic (*replacing the cheque book*) Of course. I forgot you'd be able to do things like that. Anyway, I'm not proud of what happened.

Philip I don't blame you. Forget it.

Dominic (*aggressive*) I mean, if I'd kicked *you*, at least it would seem less like just – petulance, don't you think?

Philip Yeah.

Marilyn Let's go, shall we?

Dominic (*exaggerated politeness*) No, listen, don't let me stop you doing whatever it was you were doing. Really, I mean let's be civilised.

Philip You're not stopping us doing what we're doing. But why don't we try and talk about what's happened?

Dominic You see, there's another thing which you're good at which I just can't do.

Philip What's that?

Dominic Making life into conversation. Marilyn can do it, of course. The *two* of you must have a great time – all that sponge stuff –

Marilyn For God's sake, Dominic!

Dominic Exchanging liquids. Dribbling into each other.

Philip Dominic!

Marilyn Don't get involved, Philip.

Philip It's all right. I don't feel that's what I'm doing. (*To* **Dominic**.) I don't know of any other way of communicating with you without using words. I know you're hurt. I know this hurts you. And I'm sorry. But we're in love, and we want to be together, and Marilyn's going to come and live with me in Bristol. And that directly involves you, and I want you to know about it, and if it means that we have to talk in a restaurant on a Saturday afternoon, then so be it. I don't think that ignoring the reality and playing, or whatever it is that's happening –

As **Philip** *trails off, a woman,* **Jenny,** *comes up behind* **Dominic** *and puts her hands round his eyes. Her husband,* **Malcolm,** *stands droopily behind her with* **Josephine,** *their sixteen-year-old daughter.*

Jenny   Guess who? (*Beams at* **Marilyn**.) Don't say. (**Marilyn** *doesn't say. Neither does* **Philip**. **Dominic** *has begun weeping into* **Jenny**'s *hands*.) Do you want a clue? (*She teases.*) Somebody who's very angry with you, because you promised to come and see us and show us your baby. And then you didn't come to see me in my Gilbert and Sullivan either. Is it because you're too famous now? (*She giggles. No response from* **Dominic**. **Philip** *and* **Marilyn** *are paralysed.*) And Malcolm, Malcolm saw your cartoons in *Harpers* and thought they were very wicked! Guessed? No? (*Laughing to* **Philip**.) Don't worry, I'm not from the loony bin. (*To* **Dominic**.) Come on! Guess! I'm not going to take my hands away until you've guessed who this is!

Malcolm (*uncomfortable*)   He knows. I think. (*To* **Marilyn**.) Hello.

Jenny   No, he's got to guess! (**Dominic** *shudders uncontrollably*.) Are you laughing?

Marilyn   Jenny, I really don't think this . . .

Jenny   Oh Marilyn! You've spoiled it. You –

Philip   I'm sorry but Dominic's not been feeling well. Perhaps he could call you later.

Jenny   What?

Dominic *covers his eyes with his own hands, keeps his head down.*

Malcolm   I'm sorry . . . Jenny's . . .

Philip   Please. Do you think you might – ?

Malcolm   Let's go, Jenny. I'm sorry Marilyn. We'll give you a bell.

Jenny (*cooing she's spotted the baby*)   Is that the baby? A little boy! (*To* **Marilyn**.) What do you call him?

Marilyn   Jack.

Jenny   Lovely. Well bye little Jack . . . Marilyn. (*To* **Philip**.) Nice to have met you. (*She pats* **Dominic**'s *head*.) Well, we're off. (*To* **Marilyn**.) We're buying Josephine a dress.

Marilyn   Great.

Jenny   She's going to a disco tonight. Wearing my shoes! Can you imagine! It's lovely to see you again. Bye-bye Jack. Very handsome!

The retreat is completed. **Marilyn** *and* **Philip** *sit in silence.* **Dominic** *sits, head slumped, sobbing into his hands.*

Philip (*to* **Marilyn**)   Are you going to eat any of this?

Marilyn   I'm not hungry.

Philip   Shall we have a coffee? Dominic, would you like a cup of coffee? (**Dominic** *nods in his hands.*)

Philip *gets up.* **Marilyn** *puts a comforting arm around* **Dominic**. *He keeps his head down.*

Dominic/Marilyn's *house. The next evening.*

Marilyn *is on her knees in the sitting room, sorting out books and records into two piles, hers and* **Dominic**'s. **Dominic** *returns, having put* **Jack** *to bed.*

Dominic   He was really exhausted. He almost dropped off when I was drying him after the bath. (*He kneels down by the books.*) Which pile's yours?

Marilyn   This one.

Dominic *takes a book from 'his' pile.*

Dominic   Oh. Is this mine?

Marilyn   Well . . . it was a Christmas present to us both from your aunt in Greenwich. I think that means you keep it.

Dominic   I've never looked at it. Do you want it?

Marilyn   No.

Dominic (*as they continue sorting*)   What's happening about the move?

Marilyn   Philip's coming with a van in the morning.

Dominic   Tomorrow?

Pause.

Marilyn   Yeah.

Dominic   A van full, huh?

Marilyn   There's all Jack's things. His cot, and stuff. And the highchair.

Dominic   Right.

They continue.

Marilyn   You don't have to do this, Dom. I can manage.

Dominic   It's okay. What else are you taking besides your books?

Marilyn   Oh, maybe my records. Some clothes.

Dominic   What about furniture?

Marilyn   Well, I don't know. What do you think?

Dominic (*meaning it*)   Take whatever you want.

Marilyn   Actually, the thing which I'd . . . I could really do with, but I mean, obviously if . . .

Dominic   What?

Marilyn   The bed.

Dominic (*this registers*)   Right.

Marilyn   It's just that I mean you know it's what I need for my back and the one Philip has is no good and . . .

Dominic   No, take it. (*Pause.*) I probably wouldn't be able to sleep in it again anyway.

Marilyn   It's a bed, Dominic.

Dominic   Yeah.

Marilyn   But thanks. That's kind.

Dominic   Listen, Marilyn. I don't care. It's not kindness. You're going. Jack's going. The possessions – the things in this place – are neither here nor there. If I come back tomorrow and the house is empty, it really wouldn't bother me.

Marilyn   Well obviously, there's no question –

Dominic   Oh, I'd like to keep the stereo.

Marilyn (*she wanted it*)   Okay.

Dominic   Unless you particularly . . .

Marilyn   No it's fine. Could I have the radio-cassette then?

Dominic   Fine.

Marilyn   And I would be grateful if I could have the washing machine.

Dominic (*surprised*)   Philip doesn't have one?

Marilyn   No. And there's all the baby's stuff . . . nappies and, well, you know, there's half a house to wash every day. I really couldn't manage without –

Dominic No, no. I said . . . whatever you want.

Marilyn I'd rather you knew what I was taking. And agree.

Dominic What about the car?

Marilyn I don't know.

Marilyn *wants the car. So does* **Dominic**. *He's also begun to contemplate all the other things he'd like to keep.*

Dominic Well, the thing is, if you take the car, how do I get to see Jack? (*A pause.*) That is allowed?

Marilyn Don't be stupid. You know you can see him as much as you like.

Dominic Every day? (*No response.*) Anyway, that's the problem as regards the car.

Pause.

Marilyn It's very easy by train.

Dominic Yeah, but when I get to the other end, then what?

Marilyn In what sense?

Dominic Well, do I have to say yes or no this minute?

Marilyn Well obviously not.

There's a sheet of paper on the floor. **Dominic** *picks it up, examines it.*

Dominic Is this the list of things you wanted to take with you?

Marilyn I mean, I hadn't actually intended for you to read it. It's just to jog my thoughts.

Dominic (*looking down the list*) Doesn't Philip have cutlery?

Marilyn I don't know. I don't want to be dependent on him. I'd rather have things which . . . Anyway, we got two sets from our wedding presents. You don't need them both.

Dominic No. I guess not. It's just that there are things here which I won't have but I'm sure Philip already has. The liquidiser . . . uh – the radio alarm – surely you don't want that? So you end up with two of something and . . .

Marilyn He doesn't actually have a liquidiser, but anyway.

Dominic (*putting down the list*) Look, this is silly. If I read this list I'll get . . . I'm getting frazzled here. I mean it when I say I'd prefer you just took the stuff . . . I probably won't even notice it's gone. Actually, I'll tell you what you *can* take.

Marilyn What's that?

Dominic The lawn mower.

Marilyn Why?

Dominic Haven't you got a garden in Bristol?

Marilyn Hardly.

Dominic Well, it'll come in handy.

Marilyn What about the lawn? I bought you that lawn mower.

Dominic I'll pay a boy-scout to cut it once a year.

Marilyn He'll still have to have something to cut it with.

Dominic I don't care. He can use his teeth.

Pause.

Marilyn Why didn't you say?

Dominic That I hate gardening?

Marilyn Yes.

Dominic (*slowly*)   Or decorating? Or rambles? Or holidays? Or exhibitions?

Marilyn   Yes, if you do!

Dominic   Because there's not much else, is there, of the things you enjoy?

Marilyn   How did we get to here, Dominic?

Dominic   I think that at one point we were in love. Wasn't that it?

Marilyn   I need a drink. How about you?

Dominic   I'll get it. What?

Marilyn   Anything.

Dominic   Can I say something to you, Marilyn. Since you – over the last few weeks – or perhaps I've just started looking at you . . . anyway, you look lovely. You look great. (*Pause.*) I know what we'll drink.

He springs up, goes to the cupboard and hunts. He finds an ancient bottle of champagne. Takes it, and two glasses.

Marilyn (*smiling*)   You can't resist it, can you?

Dominic   What?

Marilyn   Yes, okay, let's drink that.

Dominic   Listen, I can't see us celebrating our silver wedding anniversary together. So let's celebrate this, eh?

Marilyn   I don't mind.

Dominic   Right. (*He opens the bottle. There is no pop.*) Oh it's flat. How appropriate. (*Pours anyway.*) To . . . something.

Marilyn   To something. (*They drink.*) Will you get a lodger to move in here?

Dominic   No idea.

Marilyn   Or sell it?

Dominic   You worried about the money?

Marilyn   Not at the moment, no.

Dominic   Then I've no idea what I'm going to do. And I don't want to think about it. And the Joan Armatrading's mine, I think.

Marilyn   It's mine.

Dominic   Then there must be two copies, because I know I had one.

Marilyn (*incredulous*)   You didn't!

Dominic   Yes. I did.

Marilyn   One of the reasons you moved in with me was because I had that record!

Dominic   It was the Vivaldi I coveted.

Marilyn   And the Joan Armatrading! Christ!

Dominic   Well, you never listen to them; you take the covers, and I'll keep the records.

Marilyn (*raging now*)   Dominic, you sort out which records you want. As you're keeping the stereo it makes no odds.

Dominic (*placating*)   Hey.

Marilyn   You seem to find this easy. I don't. And I don't want to have an inquest over each thing in the house. Or be reminded that it has a history.

Dominic   Why not?

Marilyn   When did we last talk this much?

Pause.

Dominic   I don't know.

Marilyn   And why has it taken this?

She goes into the kitchen. **Dominic** *goes to the stereo and plays the Joan Armatrading record. The song is 'Love and*

Affection'. He turns the volume up loud. Pours himself another glass of flat champagne.

Dominic/Marilyn's *house: the bathroom. Later that evening.*

Marilyn *is soaking in the bath.* **Dominic** *comes in without warning. She covers herself.*

Dominic   Yes. Isn't that funny? We can't be naked. I'm sorry, I just wanted to wash your back.

Marilyn (*she moves down the bath, presenting him with her back*)   Thanks. Go ahead.

Dominic *takes a sponge and sits on the edge of the tub. He begins to wash her back, slowly, lovingly.*

Dominic   You didn't lock the door.

Marilyn   I didn't expect you to come in. You never would, even when I asked.

Dominic   Well, no.

Pause.

Marilyn   I'm sorry. (*She means for everything.*)

Dominic (*very gently*)   So am I, Marilyn. (*He kisses the centre of her back.*)

Marilyn (*embarrassed*)   Hey.

Dominic   I do love you, Marilyn. (*He kisses her again, leaning more and more into the bath, getting wet. He is fully clothed.*)

Marilyn   Don't.

Dominic   Marilyn, please. (*He embraces her from behind.*)

Marilyn (*resisting*)   Oh look, don't please. (*She clambers out, grabs a towel. As she does so,* **Dominic** *half* *slips, half flops into the bath.*) I'm sorry. I can't. I'm sorry.

She exits, embarrassed, upset. **Dominic** *stretches out in the bath.*

Dominic/Marilyn's *house. The following day.*

Dominic *arrives at the house, lets himself in.* **Marilyn** *has left. The place doesn't just feel empty:* **Marilyn** *has taken him at his word. Pictures gone, furniture. He walks from room to room as if in a trance. It is a bright winter's day and the light in the room is odd, unfamiliar. He goes into the kitchen/dining room. It is virtually bare. A lonely liquidiser on the table, the dresser denuded. He walks through to the sitting room where he and* **Marilyn** *had divided the records and books. It is particularly stark and actually quite elegant. He goes to the stereo and puts on Vivaldi's 'Stabat Mater'. He sits on the sofa, throws his head back. The music, the sunlight, flooding in.*

The M4. A Saturday soon after. Early morning.

The Beetle pop-pops towards Bristol. **Dominic** *is driving. The radio is on loud. He leaves the motorway and joins the road to Bristol.*

Two girls are standing, hitching, **Angie** *and* **Stephanie**. *Marvellous women.* **Dominic** *stops to pick them up.*

Dominic   Hello. Where d'you want to go?

Stephanie   Bristol?

Dominic   Great. Get in.

Angie *struggles to get into the back seat, the child seat is in her way.* **Stephanie** *sits in the front next to* **Dominic**.

Dominic   So. Where can I take you? I don't actually know Bristol.

Stephanie   Anywhere in the centre is fine thanks. (*Turns to* **Angie** *for confirmation.*) Yeah? (**Angie** *nods.*)

Dominic   Okay. And what, are you up for the weekend?

Stephanie   No, we live in Bristol . . . well Clifton.

Dominic   Right.

Stephanie   We went to a party in Bath. And it went on a bit. (*She laughs.*) Hence our party frocks.

You wouldn't have known that **Stephanie** *was in her party frock – not that she's dressed unattractively. It's just that she makes no concessions to High Street fashion or make-up.*

Dominic   Right.

Stephanie   How about you?

Dominic   Oh, I haven't been to a party. (*To* **Angie**.) Are you okay in the back there? I think the seat unclips if you . . .

Angie   I'm fine. You have a baby, don't you?

Dominic   Yeah. I do.

Angie   How old?

Dominic   Oh. He's just over a year, I think.

Angie (*she likes babies*)   Oh. What's his name:

Dominic   Jack. What's Bristol like?

Angie   Good.

Stephanie   Good.

Dominic   Are you students?

Stephanie   I'm not.

Angie   I am.

Dominic (*to* **Stephanie**)   What do you do?

Stephanie (*enthusiastically*)   Well, I was a student.

This is my first job, actually. I'm working at a women's advisory centre. It's great.

Dominic   It sounds great. Do they have a men's advisory centre?

Stephanie (*smiling but cool*)   No. I don't think so.

Angie (*diplomatically*)   I'm doing teacher training.

Dominic   Ah, you enjoying it?

Angie   Yeah.

Stephanie (*to* **Dominic**)   What do you do?

Dominic   Oh, I'm an entirely frivolous person. Uh, at the moment . . . What am I doing? Uh, I think I'm doing 'O' level life.

Stephanie   Is that a full-time job?

Dominic   Seems to be.

Stephanie   So you're unwaged, then?

Dominic   No, uh, I get a grant.

Stephanie   Do you not like talking about yourself?

Dominic (*thrown*)   Uh. I don't mind.

Stephanie   It's up to you. Anyway the music's good.

Dominic   Uh. What I'm doing . . . Well, my wife's just left me and moved here and I'm going to see my son. For the first time.

The girls don't know what to say. **Dominic** *turns up the music.*

Bristol. **Philip**'s *new shop. A little later.*

Dominic *has dropped off the girls and found* **Philip**'s *shop.*

The shop is not open yet. **Dominic** *peers through the window. His view is restricted by a venetian blind, but he* *can see* **Philip** *working with a saw. It is shambolic, but has the makings of a smart place. Tasteful restoration.*

Marilyn *comes in with a mug of tea for* **Philip**. *She has* **Jack** *plaited into one arm. They talk. It's inaudible through the glass, but clearly they're close. They kiss. For a second,* **Dominic** *is presented with a tableau of radiant family life:* **Philip**, **Marilyn**, **Jack**. *Then* **Marilyn** *glances at the window and sees* **Dominic**.

Bristol. The same afternoon.

Dominic *and* **Jack**'s *afternoon is a melancholy exploration of Bristol's public amenities. The highlight is the zoo.* **Jack** *is largely unimpressed. Then there's a push in the pushchair. A drive in the car. A visit to a newsagent's. And to the park, where* **Jack** *stays in his buggy, and* **Dominic** *sits on a bench. In the course of the afternoon,* **Jack** *is changed several times.*

Philip's *new flat. Simultaneously.*

Philip *comes in to find* **Marilyn** *sitting – morose – in the middle of a half-decorated room.*

Philip (*gently*)   You offered to make me a cup of tea an hour ago. (*She doesn't respond.*) Can I get you one?

Marilyn   What would you do with a baby in a city you didn't know?

Philip   He could have stayed here.

Marilyn   Would you?

Philip   I don't know. I'd go to an information centre. I don't know. Do you think there's more we could do?

Marilyn   Probably not.

Philip   Dominic's not short on ingenuity. This is the first time. He's bound to feel . . .

Marilyn   What about Jack? He was crying when they left. Oh and how many times can you patrol the same places? It's no fun for him.

Philip   Well that's true whoever takes him.

Marilyn   (*harshly*) Don't keep on having a reply please Philip.

Philip   Okay.

He walks out of the room. **Marilyn,** *repentant, goes after him.*

Marilyn   Philip. I'm sorry. (*She reaches out to him.*)

Philip (*the rebuke is forgotten*)   Do you want that cup of tea?

Marilyn *nods.*

Outside. The same afternoon.

Roaming aimlessly. **Dominic** *and* **Jack** *while away their afternoon.* **Dominic** *struggles to change* **Jack** *in the back of the Beetle.*

Philip*'s flat. Late afternoon.*

Marilyn *is lying on* **Philip***'s lap upstairs on the couch. The doorbell rings.*

Philip   I'll let them in.

Marilyn   No, it's okay. I'll go.

Marilyn *goes down and opens the door to* **Dominic** *and* **Jack.** *Mother and son practically grab each other.* **Dominic** *parks the buggy.* **Marilyn,** *feeling* **Jack,** *notices that he needs changing.*

Marilyn   Hello!

Dominic (*ferociously cheerful*)   Say 'Hi, Mum.'

Marilyn   Are you all right? Did you have a nice afternoon?

Dominic   Yeah great!

Marilyn   Was he okay?

Dominic   Yeah. We met a few people. We took in a movie. Played pool.

Marilyn (*to* **Jack**)   You look tired, darling.

Dominic   I think he is. All that fresh air.

Marilyn   Will you come in? There's food.

Dominic   No. I want to get back. While there's still some daylight.

Marilyn   Okay. (*Pauses.*) So.

Dominic   So.

Marilyn   Next weekend?

Dominic   Great.

Marilyn   Did he sleep at all?

Dominic   Not really.

Marilyn   And you found the park?

Dominic   Yeah.

Marilyn   Yeah . . . so.

Dominic (*to* **Jack**)   Well, bye-bye then.

Marilyn   Say 'Bye, Dad. Thanks for a nice afternoon'.

Dominic (*in exaggerated tones, as if talking to the baby*)   We had a milk shake.

Marilyn (*in similar tones*)   Did you! (*Pause, nothing else to say.*) Okay.

Dominic   Right . . . well I'll see you . . . next week.

Marilyn   All right. Drive safely. (**Dominic** *goes to the car. To* **Jack**.) Say 'Bye'.

Marilyn *shuts the door. She carries* **Jack** *upstairs to* **Philip**. **Philip** *has picked up on the decorating. He looks round inquiringly.*

Philip   Okay?

Marilyn (*exasperated, tearful, of* **Jack**)   He's soaked, Philip.

Dominic's *house. Sitting room. That night.*

Chris *and* **Dominic** *loll about on the floor. The television is on. Snooker. There's a bottle of wine, cutlery and glasses.* **Siobhan** *comes in with a tray full of steaming goodies.*

Chris   Mmm!

Dominic   Siobhan – you're great!

Siobhan   I know.

Dominic   You don't know how welcome this is. I'm exhausted.

Siobhan   Well, shut up and eat. And then I want to hear all about your day.

Chris (*jovially*)   Christ. Dom, I thought you'd got away from this!

Siobhan   You can shut up, too. And does anybody mind if I change this? There's a film on the other side.

Chris (*enjoying himself*)   Bloody hell.

She changes channel. They dig in happily.

Philip's *new flat. The same night. Very late.*

Jack's *room.* **Marilyn** *is holding* **Jack**, *trying to soothe him back to sleep.* **Philip** *appears sleepily, wearing pyjamas.*

Philip   No luck?

Marilyn   No. It's hopeless. He goes to sleep, I put him down, and he wakes up. He's really upset.

Philip   Do you want me to have a go?

Marilyn   No. It's all right.

Philip   Why don't you bring him to bed?

Marilyn   I think I'll have to.

Philip   Come on, then.

Marilyn   I feel like I'm sleepwalking.

All three go through to **Philip/Marilyn**'s *bed and get in.* **Jack** *in the middle. He doesn't stop crying. He won't lie down.*

Marilyn (*despairing*)   Jack. Come on!

Dominic's *house. The same night.*

The bedroom. It's fairly empty. There's a futon rolled up in one corner. **Siobhan** *and* **Dominic** *enter, holding hands. They survey the room.*

Siobhan   It's pretty austere.

Dominic   Oh yes.

Siobhan (*realising why it seems so bare*)   Dom. Where's the bed?

Dominic *unravels the futon with an impressive flourish.*

Siobhan   Dominic, you're so trendy!

Dominic   Yeah.

Siobhan   Are you drunk?

Dominic   Yeah.

Siobhan   Because this feels sort of romantic.

Dominic   Yeah.

They kiss. **Dominic** *goes to the wardrobe and pulls out the duvet stuffed inside it. Then envelops himself and* **Siobhan** *in it. The headless creature they have created moves silently to the futon and descends onto it. There's a bit of wriggling and fumbling and then* **Dominic**'s *head appears. He gets up.*

Siobhan (*apprehensive*)   Now what?

Dominic   I forgot the sheet.

He fetches the sheet from the wardrobe. In a complicated movement, he rolls **Siobhan** *and the duvet cover over to one side of the futon, covers the exposed half of the futon with the sheet, then rolls* **Siobhan** *and the duvet back to the other side, and covers the second half with the rest of the sheet. It's a remarkably slick operation. He gets in and pulls the duvet over them.*

Bristol streets. A week later. Early afternoon.

Dominic *pushing* **Jack** *along in the buggy. They pass a launderette.* **Angie**'s *sitting inside.* **Dominic** *double takes. Stops, and bangs on the window.* **Angie** *looks up, registers who it is.* **Dominic** *waves. She comes out.*

Dominic   Hello!

Angie   Hello.

Dominic   This is the boy – Jack!

Angie (*to* **Jack**)   Hello! (*Looks at* **Dominic**.) Coincidence.

Dominic   Yeah.

Angie   I thought about you last weekend. We both did. We wondered how you managed.

Dominic   Well thank you. We survived. (*To* **Jack**.) Didn't we, eh? (**Jack** *doesn't respond. To* **Angie**.) Nothing. He's sulking.

Angie   Oh. Why?

Dominic   No idea. He won't say. How's teaching?

Angie (*correcting*)   Learning to teach.

Dominic   Right.

Angie   It's fine. I thought you might not have remembered.

Dominic   Oh, I remembered. Look, uh, are you by yourself?

Angie   Yeah. Well, I'm with my laundry.

Dominic   Well, we were thinking of having a cup of coffee. So do you want to come along?

Angie   Okay.

Dominic   Great.

Angie (*she points in the direction* **Dominic** *and* **Jack** *have just been*)   There's one that way.

Dominic   Is there?

Angie   Yeah.

Dominic (*to* **Jack**)   Oi! We missed it! (*To* **Angie**.) Look, uh, look . . . I don't know your name.

Angie   Angie.

Dominic   I'm Dominic. Hello Angie.

Angie   Hello. So what did you do last week?

Dominic   Oh. Anything I could think of, really. I resorted to everything except sweets.

Angie (*laughing*)   Why not sweets? Are you against sweets?

Dominic   No. Not at all. No.

Angie   Well, you should be. If he doesn't eat sweets now, he won't want to when he's older.

Dominic   Is that so? Well, I'm afraid I can't monitor

his diet quite so closely. But anyway, not sweets because somebody I know didn't live with her father and he used to take her out at weekends and every evening after those outings she'd be really sick from chocolate and candy floss and anything else he could cram down to keep her happy.

Angie Oh dear.

Dominic Exactly.

Angie So, it was parks and swings and walks and. . . ?

Dominic Yes. All that. And a cafe and the zoo – he likes the zoo – and, uh, I can't think . . .

Angie Where will you go if it's raining?

Dominic Everybody asks me that.

Angie (*of* **Jack**) He lives near here, doesn't he?

Dominic Yes, that's right. Yeah, a couple of streets away.

Angie It's just that . . . well, so do we, and you'd be welcome to come round if you wanted. Well, if you were at a loose end. In fact, why not come now and I'll make you coffee. Steph will be really pleased to see both of you.

Dominic Steph's your mate, right?

Angie Yeah.

Dominic Well thank you. Great. (*To* **Jack**.) That's good, isn't it?

Angie He's still sulking.

Dominic Yep.

Angie Don't let me forget my laundry. Oh, what am I doing! It's this way!

They turn round and go back the way they were coming, another little family in the making.

Part Three

Dominic's *house. Morning.*

A Saturday morning some weeks on. The ritual drive to Bristol is now established. **Dominic** *is always late. Today is no exception: he hurtles out of the house, putting on his jacket as he goes, holding his toast with his teeth. He is starting the car and already has the stereo up impossibly loud, when* **Siobhan** *hurtles out after him. She is barefooted, and wearing a coat over not much else. She's carrying a bag.*

Siobhan   Dom! Dom!

She gets to the car just as he is about to pull away. **Dominic** *sees her, winds down his window and turns off the music.*

Dominic   Hi. (*Apologising for not having said goodbye.*) Sorry, but I'm late and I didn't want to wake you.

Siobhan   I know, but you forgot the present for Jack. (*She hands him the bag.*)

Dominic   Thanks. You should give it to him yourself. It's a shame.

Siobhan   I know.

Dominic   I'll try and bring him back for a weekend soon.

Siobhan   I'd like that.

Dominic   So would I Siobhan. Anyway . . . (*He makes a weary gesture: the long journey ahead of him.*) See you tomorrow.

Siobhan   Don't go back to sleep.

Dominic *turns on the stereo again. Loud.*

Dominic   Infallible.

Siobhan I may still be here when you get back. My feet are frozen to the pavement.

Dominic (*unable to hear*) What?

Siobhan (*shouting over the music*) My feet are frozen!

Dominic Oh. Sorry. (*He leans out, and they kiss fleetingly before he drives off.*)

Siobhan *watches him drive off.*

Outside **Chris**'s *house. A few minutes later.*

The VW stops outside **Chris**'s *house, it's arrival heralded by the stereo.* **Dominic** *beep-beeps to the waiting and impatient* **Chris**. **Chris** *hops in, and they set off to Bristol.*

The VW en-route to Bristol. A little later. **Dominic** *is filling* **Chris** *in with the complex upheavals of his new life as a single man.*

Dominic I'm in love, Chris.

Chris Well thank God for that. 'Cos the sackcloth and ashes routine was getting to be a right pain.

Dominic Do you like the name Celia?

Chris It's all right.

Dominic She's so beautiful. I mean, I don't know anything about her, but she's so beautiful.

Chris (*unimpressed*) Yeah. You said.

Dominic No, really. And she's so unimpressed. You know she's just . . . Totally. Totally unimpressed.

Chris Like Marilyn, you mean?

Dominic You know what I mean.

Chris No. I don't. I mean Siobhan's very impressed. Settle for that. I would.

Dominic   Well, you couldn't bullshit Celia. You just couldn't.

Chris   Yeah, well I've never been able to bullshit any women. They just say, 'That's bullshit Chris'.

Dominic   No, I really want you to meet her, Chris. You know she's made a film about Rothko?

Chris (*unsure who Rothko is*)   Is that good?

Dominic   Yeah. I think so. (*Pause. Then excited.*) Oh yeah, she takes these photographs . . . You know, it's the first time I've looked at a picture of myself and thought yes, that's me, that's what I look like.

Chris (*unexcited*)   I've never had that problem, either.

Dominic   But the thing is: what about Angie?

Chris (*struggling to keep track*)   This is Angie we're going to see in Bristol?

Dominic (*thinking of* **Angie** *now*)   She's lovely.

Chris   You know, you're like a big kid who's just discovered what his willie's for.

Dominic (*not listening still thinking of* **Angie**)   It's all very strange, Chris. What's happening. If we stayed at Angie's tonight would that bother you?

Chris (*boggled*)   Yes!

Dominic   Well . . . Celia's just sort of hypothetical. I've got high hopes for you and Stephanie.

Chris (*completely confused*)   Stephanie.

Dominic   Stephanie's great.

They drive on.

The swimming baths. The same time.

Philip, Marilyn *and* **Jack** *are in the learner's pool of a busy swimming baths.* **Philip,** *holding* **Jack,** *spins round in*

*circles, swooshing the baby in the water. He makes
aeroplane noises.* **Jack** *loves it.* **Marilyn** *looks concerned
though, and after the spin she takes* **Jack** *from* **Philip.**

Marilyn (*to* **Philip**)   You're putting on weight.

Philip (*inspecting himself*)   I'm middle-aged. It's
allowed.

Marilyn   No it's not.

Philip   Shut up, I bite.

*He ducks playfully under the surface, perhaps to bite. In
the process* **Jack** *is disturbed.*

Marilyn   Careful, Philip. Gently! (**Jack** *begins to cry.*)
You are stupid. Now look what you've done.

Philip (*weary of all this over protectiveness*)   Oh God.

Jack *screams.* **Philip** *leaves* **Marilyn** *and the baby, and
heads for the deep end.*

The coffee bar overlooking the pool. A little later.

Philip *is sitting, still a little sore from the pool episode,
drinking tea.* **Marilyn** *arrives holding* **Jack.** *She's fretful.*

Philip   Okay?

Marilyn   I think we'd better go. I don't want to be
out when Dominic arrives.

Philip   There's plenty of time. Have a drink.

Marilyn   Why did you go off like that?

Philip   I wish you'd relax about Jack. He loves the
water. He's fearless.

Marilyn   Only because I've never given him anything
to be frightened about.

Philip   No.

Marilyn   Well, yes.

Philip   Why are you taking it out on me?

Marilyn   What do you mean?

Philip   I will not be banged over the head every single day with Dominic's pain.

Marilyn   Can we just go to the car, please?

Philip *drinks his tea.*

Marilyn (*insistent*)   Please?

Philip   In a minute.

Marilyn   Can we go to the car *now*?

Philip   When I've finished my tea.

Marilyn   I'll see you there.

She is angry. She turns and leaves.

Bristol. The same time.

Dominic *and* **Chris,** *in the VW, are approaching* **Stephanie** *and* **Angie**'*s house.*

Dominic   I hate this journey. I'm always late. I hate the whole day, the whole thing.

Chris   What? Seeing Jack?

Dominic   No. Not Jack. No. The bits around him. I don't think it's him.

Chris   How's Marilyn with you?

Dominic   Okay. Cool. A bit closed. I don't know.

Chris (*facetious*)   Just the same as usual then.

Dominic   We're almost there.

Chris   Well, don't go maudlin on me. I thought you said these women were marvellous.

Dominic   They are. (**Dominic** *spots* **Stephanie** *parking her bike as they pull up outside the house.*) There's Steph.

Dominic *beep-beeps.*

The swimming baths. A staircase.

Philip, *coming down, meets a repentant* **Marilyn** *returning.* **Jack** *is in her arms.*

Philip   Sorry. I was coming.

Marilyn   No, *I'm* sorry. We were coming back. Besides, it's earlier than I thought. I want a drink. (*She nods to* **Jack.**) And so does he. Is that allowed?

Philip (*smiling*)   Yeah.

With **Jack** *squashed between them, they try to embrace. Then they turn to go back to the cafe.*

Marilyn   Philip, just a minute. (*They stop.*) I think I might be pregnant.

Philip   Oh.

Marilyn   Exactly. It's just, I feel like I am. And I'm very late. I'm hoping it's just anxiety. But I'm anxious because I don't think it is.

Philip   Then tonight can be a celebration. (*They have planned to go out while* **Philip***'s sister baby-sits.*)

Marilyn   Would you celebrate?

Philip (*smiles*)   Yes

Marilyn   Philip –

Philip (*carrying on for her*)   But do we have to go out tonight? (*Smiles*) Not if you're that worried about it. But you needn't be. Katherine's wonderful with kids. She practically brought me up. Come on, let's get you two a drink.

They move off, again, towards the cafe.

Angie *and* **Stephanie***'s house. A little later.*

Stephanie *escorts the boys into the living room.*

Stephanie   Come on in. (*They remain standing.*

Dominic *is anxious to get going.*) Well, sit yourselves down.

They do so. But **Angie** *comes in, brushing her hair, and* **Dominic** *gets up to kiss her.*

Dominic   Hello. How are you?

Angie   Okay. I was washing my hair.

Dominic   Fine. (*The time, not the hair.*)

Angie   Although I've been up for ages, eh Steph?

Stephanie   Hours. This is Chris.

Angie   Hello Chris.

Chris   Hi. I'm surprised we were allowed in, actually.

Stephanie (*explains, cheerfully*)   I think I was rude and I'm sorry. It's just habit.

Angie   Ignore her. Underneath the teeth she's all heart.

Stephanie   All bust actually. But underneath that, definitely.

Chris   Well, good.

Dominic   He's almost speechless. That's a record.

Chris   No, it's just that I'm used to women more sort of . . .

Stephanie (*sharp*)   More sort of what?

Chris (*looks to* **Dominic** *in the hope of being bailed out*)   I wish I hadn't started this. (*To* **Dominic**.) Look, I'll wait in the car, shall I?

Dominic   No, no. I want you to stay here while I go and pick up Jack.

Angie   There's no need. I'm ready now, Dom. We can go straight to the park.

Dominic   Ah well, I'd like to pick him up on my own if that's all right.

Angie Yes, of course.

Dominic (*not entirely honest*) It's just that he might be overwhelmed – by so many faces.

Angie Do you want a cup of coffee before you go?

Dominic Look, I'd love one but I'm already late actually. I'll see you all later, okay?

Angie I'll see you out.

Dominic *and* **Angie** *go out, leaving* **Chris** *and* **Stephanie** *alone.*

Chris (*referring to the incident on the way into the house*) I think what I really meant was that everything Dominic said about you was absolutely true. (*This is a compliment.*)

Stephanie (*affected archness*) Really? What was that?

Angie (*returning from seeing* **Dominic** *out*) Do you want a coffee, Chris?

Chris Uh, yes please. Thank you.

Angie Okay.

She leaves. A beat.

Chris Very nice things.

Stephanie I'm sorry?

Chris What Dominic said about you.

They're both quite shy now.

Stephanie (*laughs*) Oh right. (*Pause.*) Ditto.

Chris What?

Stephanie The things he said about you. Ditto.

Chris (*suddenly understanding*) Oh! Ditto! Right. (*He says it quietly to himself.*) Ditto.

Marilyn/Philip's *flat. A little later.*

The flat has its own access, separate from the shop.
Marilyn *opens the door to* **Dominic**.

Dominic   Sorry. There was traffic. I was going to call.

Marilyn   Will you next time? I was getting worried. It's almost midday.

Dominic (*echoing the 'almost'*)   Well it's almost 120 miles. I'm not that late.

Marilyn   I don't know why you don't take the train.

Dominic   Then you could have the car.

Marilyn   I do actually think I need it more than you. Anyway . . .

She is anxious to get the acrimony over before they go inside – so that **Philip**'s *sister doesn't see it.*

Dominic *is anxious to get in, get* **Jack** *and get going.*

Dominic   Anyway. What's Jack doing?

Marilyn   He's upstairs with Katherine.

Dominic   Who's Katherine?

Marilyn   Oh, Philip's sister. She's staying for a few days.

Dominic   How is he?

Marilyn   He's fine. He's not sleeping. But he's fine. So, are you going to eat here or out?

Dominic   Out. (*Pause.*) How are you?

Marilyn   Oh I'm fine. I haven't got a job. I don't go out. I don't know anyone. But that's my choice, so I can't complain, can I?

Dominic   No. I guess not.

Marilyn   Oh . . . (*A big event.*) Jack is walking. (*She smiles.*)

Dominic (*this hurts, but he covers it*)   He's not!
(**Marilyn** *nods, smiling*.) Really!

Marilyn   He took a few steps on Wednesday.

Dominic (*reflectively*)   Wow!

Dominic *is utterly deflated.*

Marilyn   So, what are you going to do today?

Dominic   Oh, I don't know. Usual stuff.

Marilyn   Will you try not to let him sleep in the
afternoon? It makes the evening impossible.

Dominic (*stung*)   I don't want him to sleep either, you
know. It's the only chance I get to see him. But it's
hard just to wake him up.

Marilyn   Well I have to.

Dominic   Shall we just go and see what he's up to?

Marilyn   Okay.

Dominic   Incidentally, my parents were asking if
there was any possibility of my taking him there for a
day? (*Pause.*) They haven't seen him for so long, that's
all.

Marilyn   Okay.

Dominic   I said it was early days. But – eventually.

Marilyn (*nodding*)   No, right.

They turn and rather mournfully go in.

Upstairs, **Katherine** *is holding* **Jack**.

Marilyn   Katherine, this is Dominic.

Katherine (*awkward*)   Hello.

Dominic (*awkward*)   Hi. You're Philip's sister.

Katherine   Yes, that's right.

Marilyn   I'll get his things. (*Goes out to get* **Jack's**
things.)

There's a pause. Then **Katherine** *gives* **Jack** *to*
Dominic.

Dominic (*to* **Jack**)   Hello. Hello.

Katherine   He's lovely.

Dominic   Yes.

Outside **Philip**'s *shop. A minute or two later.*

Dominic *makes his way with* **Jack** *and paraphernalia to
the car.* **Dominic** *is not very happy.*

Dominic (*as they struggle into the car*)   So you're
walking now, are you? Well you just make damn sure
you do these things on Saturdays? Okay? Okay?
(**Dominic** *gets the present from* **Siobhan**, *which is on the
back seat.*) And this is for you. It's from your Auntie
Siobhan. Let's have a look. (**Dominic** *opens the present.
It is a tiny fisherman's smock. He holds it up against*
Jack.) Pretty stylish, huh? I might wear it after you.

He straps **Jack** *into his seat.*

The zoo. Later that afternoon.

Dominic *and* **Chris** *sit on a bench. As they talk, they
watch* **Angie**, **Stephanie** *and* **Jack** *who are
wholeheartedly enjoying the zoo.*

Dominic   What do you think of Steph?

Chris   She's great.

Dominic   Pack in the typing classes. Join the
Women's Movement.

Chris   I think she'd eat me.

Dominic   Be fun, though, eh?

Angie   Angie's beautiful.

Dominic Yeah. Jack loves her.

Chris And I think you'd eat *her*. (*Pause.*) Stephanie asked me if you were seeing anyone else.

Dominic What did you say?

Chris I said: 'Huh?'

Dominic How did that go down?

Chris Not great.

Angie *and* **Stephanie** *are having fun. They shout over to* **Dominic** *and* **Chris**.

Angie Come on! Look at this.

Dominic *and* **Chris** *get up and go to see what the fuss is all about.*

Stephanie Come on! What have you two been nattering about?

Philip's *shop. Later that day.*

Dominic *is returning* **Jack** *after their day out.* **Marilyn** *and* **Dominic** *stand at the door as they talk. There are several bags at their feet:* **Jack**'s *things from the car.*

Marilyn Nice day?

Dominic Yeah.

Marilyn I'm sorry about earlier. I was . . .

Dominic I'm sorry I was late.

Marilyn Did he walk for you?

Dominic Yeah. Incredible.

Marilyn I know. (*To* **Jack**, *who is wearing the smock from* **Siobhan**.) I like this. Where did it come from?

Dominic It's great, isn't it. I got it at home.

Marilyn It's lovely. So. Did he sleep at all?

Dominic   A bit.

Marilyn   I hope he'll sleep a bit tonight as well.

Dominic   So do I.

Dominic *gives* **Jack** *to* **Marilyn**.

Marilyn   You going straight back?

Dominic   Yeah. I expect so. Do some work. Are you doing anything interesting?

Marilyn (*meaning no*)   What do you think?

Dominic   Listen, about the car –

Marilyn   It's okay.

Dominic   No, I was thinking – perhaps we could work something out.

Marilyn   Okay. Anyway. (*To* **Jack**, *whom she is feeling with concern*.) You're a bit wet, aren't you? Come on and let's get you changed.

Dominic (*hurt by the implication*)   I do change him, you know. He's had four clean nappies today: the last about an hour ago.

Marilyn   Right.

Dominic   I'll keep the wrappers in future.

Marilyn   I believe you.

A pause. **Dominic** *decides to let it go*.

Dominic (*to* **Jack**)   Bye-bye, darling. See you next weekend.

Marilyn   Say, 'Bye Dominic, thanks for a nice day.'

Dominic (*stung*)   Is that what he's going to call me? Dominic?

Marilyn   Why? What do you want him to call you?

Dominic (*incredulous, aggressive, bitter*)   How about Daddy?

A pause. The point is not lost on **Marilyn**. *She cannot answer.*

Dominic Anyway. I'll see you Marilyn.

He quickly turns, gets into the car and leaves. The emphasis on 'Marilyn' hanging unpleasantly behind him. She watches him drive off **Jack**, *soaking, in her arms.* **Philip** *emerges from the shop. He says nothing, but starts picking up the debris to carry indoors.*

A Chinese Restaurant. Later the same evening.

The restaurant is crowded. **Chris** *and* **Dominic**, **Stephanie** *and* **Angie** – *the girls changed, the boys scrubbed* – *are squashed into a booth where they prepare to eat.* **Dominic** *is distracted, depressed.*

Chris (*to* **Dominic**) Hey.

Dominic What?

Chris Exactly. What?

Dominic I'm sorry. I'm tired. Long day. (*Leans over to the girls.*) How are you two?

Angie Fine.

Stephanie Fine thanks, dad. Can we play again next weekend?

Dominic (*not joining in*) I expect so.

Chris Now listen, when this food arrives, there are to be no knives and forks. Agreed?

Angie Well . . . I can't use chopsticks.

Chris Nor can I. Can you, Dom?

Dominic No. Not really.

Stephanie I can knit. That's similar.

Angie I can knit.

Chris   Well, there you are then: you two have got an advantage before we even start. (*Thinks.*) Although I fail to see what knitting's got to do with it.

Stephanie (*doubtfully*)   Two long thin things.

Chris   No, look, my theory is if none of us can do it, there's no problem. Because then we can all learn together without somebody scoffing the lot.

Stephanie   But I'm starving!

Chris (*enjoying himself*)   Well, there's your incentive, then.

Stephanie   Okay.

Angie   Okay.

Chris (*to* **Dominic**)   Okay?

Dominic   Yeah.

Chris   Good-o.

Marilyn *and* **Philip** *come into the restaurant, dressed up. A celebration, but also intimate, romantic.*

Marilyn   Do you think I should just ring Katherine to see if she's all right?

Philip   No. I don't. I've given her the number. What I think you *should* do, is relax.

They are seated by a polite but fantastically busy waiter. They don't see **Dominic**'*s table.*

Marilyn (*opening the menu*)   I'd forgotten what it's like to be out.

Philip   You look wonderful.

Marilyn   I feel ancient.

Philip   You *are* ancient.

Marilyn (*relaxing*)   Well, thank you. (*She laughs.*)

Philip   Will you marry me?

Marilyn   No, I'm married already.

Philip   But apart from that?

Marilyn   Why?

Philip   Because I want you to marry me.

Marilyn   But why marriage?

Philip   Why not?

Marilyn   Why repeat something that both of us have got wrong before?

Philip   Well, what if you are pregnant?

There are squeals of laughter from **Dominic**'s *table. The chopsticks have become the source of great hilarity.* **Philip** *looks over briefly. Double-takes.*

Philip   Isn't that Chris Caldwell? And Dominic?

At the same time, something makes **Dominic** *look over at* **Marilyn** *and* **Philip**'s *table. He double-takes. Freezes. Without thinking, he puts down his chopsticks and picks up a fork. Prods his food.*

Marilyn (*quickly*)   Philip, I want to go.

Chris (*following* **Dominic**'s *stare*)   Dominic –

Dominic   She said she never went out.

Angie (*still playing the chopsticks game*)   Dom! You're cheating!

Dominic   Yeah.

Stephanie   What's going on?

Chris   Are you going to go over?

Dominic   No. I want to leave, actually. Does anybody mind?

The girls don't know what's going on.

Stephanie   Yes we do!

Dominic   Well, why don't you three finish the meal?
I'll meet you outside or something.

Angie (*concerned*)   I'll come with you, Dom.

Dominic   No. Please. (*The last thing he wants*
Marilyn *to see*.) Really, you eat. (*He gets up from his
seat.*)

Chris   They're going.

Dominic   Oh shit.

Dominic *and* **Chris** *watch as* **Marilyn** *and* **Philip**
leave. **Philip** *mutters something to the waiter (who's come
to take their order) as they go. They don't acknowledge*
Dominic *or* **Chris**.

Dominic   Shit.

Dominic's *bedroom. Saturday morning, a week later.*

The bedroom is still spartan (as is the whole house.)
Dominic *is rather cultivating the austerity look.*
Dominic *and* **Siobhan** *are in bed. (The futon.) He opens
an eye and checks his watch. He's overslept. He curses,
then unravels himself elaborately from the sleeping*
Siobhan. *He hunts for clothes, noisily.* **Siobhan** *stirs.*

Siobhan   What time is it?

Dominic   Late.

Siobhan   Oh.

Dominic (*annoyed*)   Yeah: oh.

Siobhan   What time should you be there?

Dominic   Now. I don't know. Basically now.

Siobhan (*suddenly enthusiastic*)   Hey. I'd quite like to
come. Could I?

Dominic   That would be nice, but I really have to go
now.

Siobhan   I could be ready in a couple of minutes.

Dominic (*pulling on some trousers*)   No. It's more than that, it's like . . . (*He turns and explains gravely.*) It's not a good thing, these visits. I don't feel good about them. Also I want to have a clear time with the baby, I don't know, uncluttered.

Siobhan (*dropping it*)   Okay.

Dominic   Do you know what I mean, though?

Siobhan   Sure.

Dominic   It's already confusing for him without . . . (*He trails off.*) Whatever.

Siobhan   Yes.

Dominic   I mean, obviously, at some stage. I for one would like the company. If only for the drive. Look, I have to go now, I'm sorry. (*He kisses her.*)

Siobhan   See you tonight.

Dominic (*thrown*)   Uh. Well . . . I was thinking I might possibly stop over. Look, why don't we say if I'm back I'll come over to you?

Siobhan (*smiles*)   Okay. Let's say that.

Dominic   Okay. Go back to sleep now.

Siobhan   Drive carefully.

Dominic   Thanks.

He pecks her again, and dashes out. **Siobhan** *lies back in the bed. She's unhappy.*

Marilyn/Philip'*s bedroom. The same morning.*

Marilyn, Philip *and* **Jack** *are in bed, all squashed up.* **Philip** *has made some toast and stuff. He reads a novel,* **Jack** *plays,* **Marilyn** *muses.*

Marilyn   Are you sure you don't mind?

Philip   That's a trick question.

Marilyn   How come?

Philip (*cheerfully*)   Well, can a man safely mind his woman going to a women's conference?

Marilyn (*cheerfully*)   *His* woman?

Philip   Shut up. Anyway I don't. I'd like to go myself.

Marilyn   Well you can't, can he Jack?

Philip   What I'm really sore about is that I'll miss an hour in bed *by ourselves* this afternoon. (*To* **Jack**.) By ourselves! (*To* **Marilyn**.) Remember that curious sensation?

Marilyn   You tell him to sod off, Jack. You came first.

Philip   Well I hope you're not pregnant. The mind boggles.

Marilyn   The family bed!

Philip   Ugh! I'll go and sleep in the cot.

Marilyn   We could get another cot and both sleep in them, and they could come in our bed.

Philip   Or better still, get a double cot.

Marilyn (*solemn*)   You're sure you don't mind handing him over to Dominic?

Philip   No, that's fine.

Marilyn   I'd really have liked to have taken him with me.

Philip   Why didn't you arrange that? Dominic could have come tomorrow.

Marilyn   I don't want to be awkward.

Philip   It's not being awkward to rearrange the day.

Marilyn   Okay, well I don't want to be selfish then.

Philip Better to be selfish than to be self-righteous about losing out on what you really want.

Marilyn You think?

Philip Yes. I do.

Marilyn Anyway, it's important for Jack to have a routine. It's important for Dominic, too. (*Thinks.*) Do you think he's having a 'thing' with one of those girls?

Philip (*putting down his book*) Ah!

Marilyn What do you mean, 'ah'?

Philip The taboo subject.

Marilyn Not at all. Why do you say that?

Philip We see Dominic with some women a week ago and you never mention it. That seems to me to make it taboo.

Marilyn They were both too young, anyway.

Philip Why?

Marilyn I know which one it was. I know just what he goes in for.

Philip (*astonished*) God!

Marilyn It was the black one with the doe eyes. (*That's* **Angie**.)

Philip How do you know?

Marilyn Because I do. Of course, if we wait a month we can always find out from reading his bloody cartoon strip.

Philip Well, you're not black, and you certainly haven't got doe eyes.

Marilyn You can lose doe eyes.

Philip (*teasing*) Really?

Marilyn And you can shut up.

Philip   I find it hard to think of you as ever having
doe eyes.

Marilyn   Have you ever had *black* eyes?

Philip   Jack, bite your mother.

They fight in bed, happily. Spilling the things.

Angie/Stephanie's *house. The same morning.*

The bathroom. **Angie**'s *inside, washing her hair.*
Stephanie's *outside.*

Stephanie   Can I come in?

Angie   Go away.

Stephanie   What are you doing?

Angie   I'm washing my hair.

Stephanie   Well, let me in. I'm dying for a pee.

Angie   Hang on. Sorry.

Angie *unlocks the door, and* **Stephanie** *rushes in and sits
on the lavatory.* **Angie** *is leaning over the bath, rinsing
her hair with a plastic shower attachment.*

Stephanie   Do you have to wash your hair every
Saturday?

Angie   Yes.

Stephanie   I'm annoyed.

Angie   I know.

Stephanie   With both of you.

Angie   Yes.

Stephanie   Are you listening?

Angie   Yes. (*She turns off the water, turns and faces*
Stephanie.) You're annoyed with both of us.

Stephanie   Come to the conference.

Angie I'll come to the stuff tomorrow.

Stephanie (*still sitting on the lavatory*)   No. You should come both days.

Angie I don't know. Perhaps Dom'll want to bring Jack. Then we can all come.

Stephanie It's not really for men.

Angie Why not?

Stephanie Because men have conferences all the time. Because they get opportunities to talk about these things together at their places of work. Women are partitioned. Why am I telling you this? You know why.

Angie It says men can go.

Stephanie (*correcting*)   It says men can go if they're going to the single parent session.

Angie Well, he is a single parent.

Stephanie Well, he isn't actually. Marilyn is.

Angie Why do you call her Marilyn? You don't know her.

Angie *is upset, vulnerable. A pause.* **Stephanie** *flushes the lavatory.*

Stephanie Angie.

Angie What?

Stephanie Why do you only see Dominic at weekends?

Angie (*humiliated but stubborn*)   Because he probably sees somebody else.

Stephanie Yes, he probably does.

Angie So why should that stop me washing my hair?

Stephanie What does he say about it?

Angie Nothing.

Stephanie   Don't you ask?

Angie   There's no time.

Stephanie   You have sex with him. Isn't there time to talk?

Angie (*quiet*)   No. (*She pours some conditioner and begins to massage it in.*)

Stephanie   That's why you should come. (*Pause.*) Angie. It would be really good for you. You could put what's happening to you in some kind of context. With other women.

Angie   What do you mean, 'what's happening to me'? I happen to it too. I want it to happen

Stephanie (*unconvinced*)   Do you?

Angie (*stubborn*)   And to see Jack, yes. I do actually. I know what's happening.

Stephanie (*suddenly*)   Is that my conditioner?

Angie   Yeah.

Stephanie (*rushing over from the loo*)   Give us it back! (*She grabs the shower attachment, and rinses* **Angie**'s *hair, laughing.*)

Angie (*shrieking, laughing*)   Steph! Get off!

They battle for a few seconds, and **Stephanie** *gets as much of the spray as* **Angie**. *Then the moment is gone.* **Stephanie** *drops the shower attachment and gently rubs* **Angie**'s *back. They are close.* **Angie** *is weeping.* **Stephanie** *holds her.*

Philip's *flat. Midday, Saturday.*

Philip *comes into the sitting room carrying* **Jack**. *He's pursued by a breathless, contrite* **Dominic**.

Philip   Come in.

Dominic   I'm late.

Philip   It's okay.

Dominic   I can't believe I'm this late again.

Philip   Marilyn's not here.

Dominic   Oh.

Philip   She's gone to a conference. (*Not entirely honest.*) She waited but you –

Dominic   Right. (**Dominic** *is sullen. Visibly uncomfortable.*) Lots of traffic.

Dominic *approaches* **Philip,** *and virtually pulls* **Jack** *out of his arms.*

Dominic (*to* **Jack**)   Hello.

Philip (*making an effort*)   He's really growing up, isn't he? (*No response.*) Still not sleeping much, though. Has Marilyn said? But he's terrific.

Dominic (*aggressive*)   I really don't want him to call you Daddy. You know? (*Pause. Nothing from* **Philip.** **Dominic** *is in a dangerous, violent mood.*) Are you going to get married?

Philip   I've no idea.

Dominic   Christ. Well, that's one thing to be said for my son growing up with you: I'm sure he'll be able to sell things.

Philip (*civil*)   Do you need to take anything with you? A change of clothes.

Dominic (*mock civility*)   We could always play squash again, Philip.

Philip   I don't think so.

Dominic   No, I don't think so, either.

Dominic *goes to leave.*

Philip What I do think is that maybe you feel you're the only person who suffers.

Dominic (*turning, coming back in*) I'm sorry. I didn't know it hurt, living with my wife and with my child.

Philip I know you didn't.

Dominic (*slowly*) Well, if it's such a drag, Philip, send them back.

Philip They don't belong to anyone.

Dominic (*quiet, menacing*) Fuck off, Philip, please.

Dominic *leaves, clutching* **Jack.**

Angie's *bedroom. The same afternoon.*

The curtains are closed. **Dominic,** *dressed only in trousers, eases himself into bed alongside the sleeping* **Angie.** *She wakes.* **Dominic** *is easy.* **Angie** *isn't.*

Dominic You fell asleep.

Angie Did I?

Dominic I've been travelling between the two of you. (*He means her and* **Jack,** *who is asleep in the sitting room.*) You both looked so peaceful.

Angie Is he still asleep?

Dominic Yes. I'll wake him. I just wanted a few minutes with you.

Angie I must go.

Dominic You're funny.

Angie I don't think I'm funny.

Dominic I didn't mean funny.

Angie Will you come with me?

Dominic I don't think the baby's into feminism just yet. He prefers the swings.

Angie   There's an adventure playground there.

Dominic   You go. (*Easy.*) We'll go to the park. It's no problem.

Angie   I didn't say it was a problem. It would have been nice for me.

Dominic (*distracted suddenly, as if he heard* **Jack**)   Hang on. (*Listens.*) Sorry, go on.

Angie   I'll have to be applying for jobs soon.

Dominic   Oh. Right. (*Wary, but covering it.*)

Angie (*carefully*)   Is there any point in my applying for one near you?

Dominic   Well I should have thought – with the shortage of jobs – you should just apply for the job rather than the place. (*Pause.*) So, obviously, if there's one near me . . . (*Pause.*) Is there one?

Angie   I don't know. (*Pause. Bleakly.*) I really like you. Dominic. Do you know that?

Dominic   Yes.

Angie   And Jack.

Dominic   I'm sorry. (*Pause.*) I'm sorry. (*He looks down.*)

Angie (*sitting up*)   What for?

Dominic   Would you rather we stopped coming?

Angie   No.

Dominic *rolls onto his stomach.*

Dominic   Do you know what I'd really like?

Angie   What?

Dominic   For you to lie on my back.

A long pause. Then **Angie** *lies on his back. She is naked.*
It's wonderful.

Angie   Why do you like this?

Dominic   I don't know. I feel . . . I like the weight. I feel protected. If you're a man, it's a really unusual position.

Angie   I could hit you.

Dominic   Yes. You could. (*In that position.*)

Angie   No, I mean I want to hit you.

Dominic   Oh.

She thumps his back. Really hard. It doesn't make her feel any better. She rolls off and stares into space. **Dominic** *is startled.*

The park. A little later.

Dominic *pushes* **Jack** *on a swing. He sings to* **Jack**.

A girl, **Theresa**, *is playing at the next swing. She's nine or ten. Her younger brother is climbing the steps of the slide nearby. They're urchins, dirty, hard, cheeky, great.*

Theresa (*watching* **Dominic** *push* **Jack**)   Where's his mum?

Dominic   What?

Theresa   You on the dole?

Dominic   No. Why?

Theresa   What's his name?

Dominic   Jack. What's yours?

Theresa   My dad looked after us when he was on the dole. I had to cook. He didn't know how. He thinks sausages is cooking. Can you cook?

Dominic   No.

Theresa   My name's Theresa. (*Nods in the direction of her brother and the slide.*) And he's Darren.

Dominic   My name's Dominic.

Theresa   There's a girl at our school called Dominic.

Dominic   Well, there you go, eh? (*Pause.*) Boy at my school called Theresa.

Theresa   Bet there wasn't.

Dominic   There was actually.

Theresa   You married?

Dominic   Yep.

Theresa   Where's your ring then?

Dominic   Men don't wear wedding rings.

Theresa   Yes they do.

Dominic   Well, I don't wear a wedding ring because, uh, I don't live with Jack's mother any more.

Theresa (*unabashed*)   What, you divorced?

Dominic   No.

Theresa   Gonnna be?

Dominic (*not amused*)   What are you going to do when you grow up? Psychiatry?

Theresa (*doesn't know the word*)   No.

Darren (*coming over*)   I can swing on this upside down.

Theresa   No you can't. (*To* **Dominic**.) Shall I push him?

Dominic   Okay. Be careful.

Theresa (*indignant*)   I know how to push swings. (*She takes over from* **Dominic**.) You got a girlfriend?

Dominic   No. You got a boyfriend?

Theresa   No. (*Of* **Jack**.) He's wet through, in't he?

Dominic   Where? (*Lifts* **Jack** *out of the swing and inspects him anxiously. He's very wet.*) Oh.

Theresa   Better get him changed.

Darren, *attempting ambitious gymnastics, falls off the swing. No tears.* **Theresa** *goes to him.*

You stupid moron! Come on. Let's have a look at you. (*To* **Dominic**.) I'll have to get him home and all. If he bleeds, it takes ages for it to stop. Somethin' wrong with him. See you. Bye Jack.

Dominic (*to* **Jack**)   Say 'Bye-bye'.

Theresa *and* **Darren** *leave, the boy limping.*

Dominic   Oh Jack, I'm sorry. Come on, let's get you sorted out. Come on.

He puts **Jack** *into his buggy, and hurries with him across the park to the car.*

Back of **Philip**'s *shop. The same day. Dusk.*

Philip's *hanging out the washing on the roof. On the street below,* **Dominic**'s *Beetle drives up.* **Dominic** *gets out.* **Philip** *calls from the roof.*

Philip   Dominic, Marilyn's not back yet.

Dominic   That's okay.

Philip   Why don't you come up for a drink?

Dominic   Jack's asleep. (**Jack** *is in his child's seat in the car.*)

Philip   That's okay. Leave him in the car. We can watch him from up here.

Dominic *goes up the iron steps (it's a fire escape.) to the rooftop.*

Dominic   Listen, I'm sorry about this morning.

Philip (*still hanging the washing*)   Yeah, I'm sorry too.

Dominic   After all that he got soaked and I had to buy him an entire wardrobe.

Philip   You should have brought him back.

Dominic   Well.

Philip   Apart from that, was it a good day?

Dominic   Yes, it was fine.

Philip   Listen, I've still got some more washing to do. (*He indicates the basket.*) So if you've got any of Jack's things, I'll bung them in.

Dominic   Uh. No, I've left them back at the house. (*Checking himself.*) The room.

Philip   That's okay.

Dominic   I mean I've washed them. Well, I put them in to soak. I'm not very good at washing. I'm more of an ironing man, myself.

Philip   With me it's the opposite. I love hanging out the clothes.

Dominic (*mock horror*)   Terrible! (*Pause.*) No, listen, what I said earlier was uncalled for. (*Genuine apology.*)

Philip   Forget it. (*Genuine acceptance.*)

Dominic   I've been thinking how much more beautiful Marilyn looks since she's been living here.

Philip (*thinking*)   She always was, I think. (*He is struggling with a large sheet.*)

Dominic   Can I give you a hand?

Philip   No, it's okay. Why don't you go and check on Jack?

Dominic   Right.

He smiles at **Philip** *and goes back down the steps.*

Outside **Angie/Stephanie**'s *house. A little later.*

Dominic *drives up to see* **Chris** *outside the house.* **Chris** *was not expected.*

Chris   Hi. Where is everybody?

Dominic   What are you doing here?

Chris   I'm doing a chopsticks course. Where's the family?

Dominic   Jack's gone home. The girls are at a conference. So's Marilyn, as it happens. It's a women's conference.

Chris   I see. So. They can compare notes.

Dominic   Yeah. That's what I thought. (*A shade impatient.*) What are you doing here?

Chris   Stephanie and I are going Chinesing. I thought you and Angie were coming too.

Dominic   Chris – Celia's staying with me tonight. I mean, that's the . . . she's coming over, so . . .

Chris   Oh.

Dominic   Yeah. Oh.

Chris   Well, it doesn't matter if we eat, does it?

Dominic   Christ. What am I playing at? What am I doing?

Chris (*cheerful*)   I don't know. That's what Stephanie asked me. That's what Siobhan asked me. I expect Angie will ask me later on. Marilyn hasn't got my new phone number, has she? Oh, and I don't know Celia yet.

Dominic   Shut up. When did Siobhan ask you? (*Sighs. Notices* **Angie** *and* **Stephanie** *approaching.*) Christ, here they come.

Stephanie   Thanks for giving us a lift.

Dominic What?

Stephanie You passed us.

Dominic I'm sorry. I must have been miles away.

Angie Hello Chris. (*She doesn't say hello to* **Dominic**.)

Chris Hi. Hi. Steph. How was your thing?

Stephanie (*brightly*) Terrific. In fact we decided on the way home we're giving up men.

Angie *catches* **Dominic**'s *eye and looks down.*

Chris (*unperturbed*) When? 'Cause I bought you both a present.

Stephanie Soon. Probably.

Chris Oh, 'soon probably'. That's all right then. These are for you. (*He presents, with a flourish, ornamental black chopsticks. Four pairs.*) Dominic's taking his back.

Angie Oh?

Dominic Yeah, I've got people staying tonight.

Angie Oh.

Dominic I can't really duck out. (*He twiddles his chopsticks.*) I promise I'll practise at home.

Nobody speaks for a moment. It is tense.

Stephanie I'm going in. Is anybody else?

Dominic Perhaps I'd better just go straight off.

Stephanie Okay. Chris?

Chris I'd like to. Can I?

Stephanie Possibly.

Chris See you, Dom.

Stephanie *and* **Chris** *go in.*

Angie Steph and me are going to the Isle of Wight next weekend.

A beat.

Dominic Great. Well, should I ring during the week and possibly discuss the following Saturday?

A beat.

Angie (*quietly; a trace of bitterness, a trace of regret*) It's up to you. (*She turns to go in.*)

Dominic (*very gently*) I hope the Isle of Wight's nice. (*Pause.*) See you, then.

Angie Bye.

Dominic *stands by the gate, watching her go in.*

Dominic'*s house. That night.*

Dominic *enters, concerned because there is a hall light on. The place is immaculate, polished. He walks cautiously, not sure what's happened. As he passes the door of the sitting room,* **Siobhan** *speaks. She's been sitting on the sofa with some books for her research, waiting for him to return.*

Siobhan Dom?

Dominic Siobhan? What's going on?

Siobhan (*smiling*) I thought I'd spring-clean. Hi. You're back.

Dominic Why?

Siobhan Why spring-clean? Because there were things growing in your cupboard. Because, with no furniture to settle into, the dust was getting aggressive.

Dominic No look, I thought we'd arranged that if I came home I'd come to you?

Siobhan Well, now there's no need. 'Thank you

Siobhan for spending all day cleaning.' 'It's a pleasure.'
(*She curtseys.*)

Dominic (*aggressive*)   I don't need a domestic. I tried
that. I wasn't good at it.

Siobhan (*stung*)   Right.

Dominic (*calming, but still irritated*)   No, of course,
thank you. Thank you. I just feel embarrassed.

Siobhan   Well don't. Feel affectionate. Feel sexy, if
you like. (*She cuddles him.*) Shall I run a bath? You look
worn out.

Dominic (*frozen in her arms*)   Actually, the reason I
came back was because I had this sudden flash I'd said
I'd put some people up for the weekend.

Siobhan   Okay. Are you worried about feeding them?

Dominic   Feeding her.

Siobhan   Are you worried about feeding her?

A beat.

Dominic   No.

Siobhan *unravels herself from the embrace.*

Siobhan   Well you can't say fairer than that.

*She picks up her books and leaves. The sound of the front
door closing.*

Dominic's *house. Later the same night.*

Dominic – *bathed and changed – is preparing the table
for a meal. It is carefully laid. He puts a bowl of spinach,
avocado and egg salad in the middle. In the bowl are his
chopsticks: impromptu salad servers. He uncorks a bottle
of wine. He surveys the table. It looks good.*

The telephone rings. He goes into the hall to answer.

The telephone is on the table in the hall where **Dominic** *and* **Marilyn** *used to keep their joint diary. Above the table is a notice-board. A clutter of reminders, drawings and cards. Photographs of* **Jack** *including one of him wearing the fisherman's smock and* **Angie**'s *hands in evidence. One of* **Dominic** *taken by* **Celia**: *odd, quirky, stylish. Another one, cut from a magazine, of* **Celia**. *It is deliberately concealed by a large notice. As* **Dominic** *talks on the phone, he takes out the drawing pins, revealing* **Celia**'s *photograph.*

Dominic   Hello. Yes. Speaking. (*Excited when he realizes who it is.*) Hi, hi Celia! What's the matter – you got lost. (*Pause.*) What? (*Pause. Less excited.*) Oh. (*Pause.*) No, nothing, don't worry about it. (*Pause.*) No, no, no. (*Pause.*) No, I had a salad. No. (*Pause.*) Don't worry. I'll feed it to the cat. (*Pause.*) So. How about next weekend? (*Pause.*) Okay. (*Pause.*) I did. I have an intimate relationship with your answerphone. Did you get my letter? Well, you should be very flattered. I'm normally a 'two lines, love Dominic' man. Yes. (**Celia** *is called away.*) Oh, right. Well, shall I ring you back? (*Pause.*) Oh. (*Pause.*) Okay. Yeah, you too. Bye-bye.

He replaces the receiver. Realising that she hasn't registered his interest in the slightest, he sits gloomily on the stairs.

Marilyn/Philip's *bedroom. The same night.*

Marilyn *enters from the bathroom. She's surprised to see* **Philip** *in bed: it means* **Jack** *has gone to sleep.*

Philip   He's asleep.

Marilyn   I don't believe it. What did you do? Hit him over the head?

Philip   Only a couple of times.

Marilyn   Well, I don't know how you do it.

Philip (*explains*)   I've got no breasts and I sing badly:

he gets bored. (*They both smile.*) Tell me about the conference.

Marilyn   It was great. Tell me about Dominic.

Philip   No, I want a blow by blow account. Great's not good enough. Dominic was fine.

Marilyn *sits on the bed. Then cuddles him, her head on his chest. They're close. In love.*

Marilyn   Oh, by the way. I'm not pregnant.

Philip   Oh.

Marilyn *looks up just too late to see the disappointment on his face. She gives him a kiss.*

Siobhan's *house. The next day (Sunday). Early evening.*

Siobhan *opens the door on a penitent* **Dominic**. *She is appropriately unwelcoming. They stand on the doorstep.*

Dominic   I got stood up. (*No response.*) Do you want to share a salad? (*He holds up a shopping bag.*)

Siobhan   No, thanks. (*Pause.*) Do I want to share you? No, thanks.

Dominic (*honest*)   That figures. Listen Siobhan, I wanted to say a few things . . . (*He can't think how to say them.*) I mean, well I've been seeing someone in Bristol . . . uh . . .

Siobhan   I know.

Dominic   Do you?

Siobhan   Chris told me. He didn't tell me, but he couldn't say no when I asked.

Dominic   Right. I'm not going to be able to say anything, am I?

Siobhan   Not today, Dom. No.

Dominic   Tomorrow?

Siobhan   I doubt it, Dom.

Dominic   Tuesday? Wednesday? Stop me, you know, if I'm getting warm. (*Nothing.*) Next weekend? (*Nothing.*) Right. (*He retreats to the gate.*)

Siobhan (*meaning it*)   Take care.

Dominic (*meaning it*)   Yeah. And you.

He watches as she shuts the front door.

Dominic's *house. A Wednesday some weeks later.*

If anything the house is even more stark. **Dominic** *has jettisoned virtually all of the furniture.* **Jack** *is asleep in his buggy in the hall.* **Marilyn** *sits at the table in the kitchen/dining room.* **Dominic** *enters with a box.*

Dominic   I keep forgetting to bring these back.

Marilyn (*examining the contents*)   What is it?

Dominic   Well, various bits of junk, really. It's yours, not mine, though. I'll shove it in the car for you.

Marilyn   Okay. Though I don't know where it's all going to go.

Dominic   Well.

Marilyn   Seems a bit ridiculous.

Dominic   What?

Marilyn   The house. It's so empty. And the place in Bristol's not really big enough. What have you done with the sofa?

Dominic (*smiles*)   Oxfam.

Marilyn (*smiles*)   That's where it came from.

Dominic   That's where it's gone back to.

Marilyn *gets up and walks through to the sitting room.* **Dominic** *follows.*

Dominic   Don't let me forget to give you the documents for the car.

Marilyn   Right. Thanks.

Dominic   I think you'll have to get someone to look at the exhaust.

Marilyn   Right. (*She moves to the window. Looks at the house opposite.*) Do you see much of Frank and Annabel?

Dominic   Oh no. Nothing. Well, no: at first they came over. They asked for your address. Did they write?

Marilyn   Yes. A card. It was kind.

Dominic   Yeah. I sometimes see Frank. You know, he has this habit of materialising every time a woman comes within twenty feet of the house. (*Laughs. A pause.*) Oh yeah, and I had some of their home-made wine, which I gave to my father. I think he gives it to someone else.

Marilyn   Oxfam.

Dominic (*smiles*)   Probably. (*Pause.*) Well. This is terribly normal. (*He means the conversation.*)

Marilyn   Is that a regular event?

Dominic   What's that?

Marilyn   Women coming within twenty feet of the house.

Dominic   Um . . . it happens.

Marilyn   The girl from the restaurant?

Dominic   No. (*Pause.*) No. (*Pause.*) You're right – this house is ridiculous. I wanted to empty it and I've forgotten why. Anyway, I'm going to sell it. I'm going to move. (*Pause.*) Because there's no chance of you coming back.

Marilyn   No. I don't think there is.

Dominic   You know, what's funny is that you and Philip seem the couple now. I tried to imagine you naked the other day. I couldn't. (*Pause.*) Or touching you. (**Jack** *cries.*) We have a waking baby, I think.

Marilyn   I'll go. (*As she goes out to the hall.*) I thought I was pregnant again.

Dominic   Oh. Are you?

Marilyn (*coming back with* **Jack** *in her arms*)   No.

Dominic (*cooing*)   Here he is!

Marilyn   Say, 'Hello, Dad.'

Dominic (*after a beat*)   D'you fancy a walk, Marilyn?

Marilyn   Uh. Where?

Dominic   I don't know. The park.

Marilyn   Okay.

The park. A little later.

Dominic *and* **Marilyn** *push* **Jack** *into the park. It is busy. Mostly just mums and kids.*

If you were watching from a distance, you'd see a happy couple with their child. Laughing about something. The father pulling the baby out of the pushchair, sitting him on one end of the see-saw, and holding him while mother and child gently bump and rise alternately. You'd see the mother getting on the roundabout with the baby. The father pushing them round. Then jumping on himself. Then showing off, holding on with only one hand and leaning out as the roundabout turns.

And round and round they spin.

Truly, Madly, Deeply

for Juliet Stevenson

Truly, Madly, Deeply opened in the USA and the UK in 1991, with the following cast, in order of appearance:

Nina	Juliet Stevenson
Burge	Jenny Howe
Translator	Carolyn Choa
Sandy	Bill Paterson
Titus	Christopher Różycki
Plumber	Keith Bartlett
George	David Ryall
Maura	Stella Maris
Harry	Ian Hawkes
Claire	Deborah Findlay
Jamie	Alan Rickman
Frenchman	Vania Vilers
Roberto	Arturo Venegas
Symonds	Richard Syms
Mark	Michael Maloney
Isaac	Mark Long
Freddie	Teddy Kempner
Pierre	Graeme Du-Fresne
Bruno	Frank Baker
Anthony	Tony Bluto
As themselves	Members of the Reach Group, Swindon
Midwife	Heather Williams
Maura's Baby	Henry James

Designer Barbara Gosnold
Editor John Stothart
Original music Barrington Pheloung
Featured music J S Bach
Director of Photography Remi Adefarasin
Executive Producer Mark Shivas
Producer Robert Cooper
Director Anthony Minghella

A BBC Films Production presented by The Samuel Goldwyn Company.

Ext: London underground. Night.

Nina *emerges from a tube station and sets off into the night.*

Ext: London streets and **Nina**'s *flat. Night.*

Nina *is walking quickly down some alleyway steps. It's night.*

Nina *feels threatened by stray noises, footsteps, the dark. She crosses the Archway Bridge. She walks down a street.*

Nina (*VO*)   Mostly when I'm walking, at night, or anyway, alone, if I'm frightened, then he'll turn up, he'll, he'll talk, about what I'm doing, you know, some advice, he'll say – 'Don't be frightened. I've told you – walk in the middle of the road at night'.

She goes into the middle of the road.

And I will, I move over to the middle of the road, or, I don't know, he'll say – 'It's a disgrace, this street is a disgrace, there's no proper lighting, have you written, you must write!' He's always forthright, I mean he always was forthright so I suppose that's not, but, you know, he'll also speak in Spanish to me, which is odd because he couldn't speak Spanish – and I would have been feeling low, you know, very alone and hopeless and – and then he's there, his presence, and it's okay, it's fine, and I don't mind and he tells me he loves me.

She's at the front gate of the building which contains her flat. She opens the gate and goes inside.

And then he's not there anymore.

Burge (*VO*)   And then how do you feel?

Nina (*VO*)   Okay, fine, well, I feel looked after, I suppose, watched over. You see, he never says anything profound or earth-shattering, you know, he doesn't say *well God thinks this* or –

Int: Therapist's room. Day.

Grey sky outside the window. Camera pushes down to
Nina *who is sitting on a heavy armchair, next to a*
Georgian picture window.

Her therapist **Burge** *presides.*

Nina – or about the planet or world events or, or
there's no God, or, it's all *go to bed, brush your teeth,* or
the way I'm brushing my teeth, because I always brush
them side to side and I'll be doing that and he'll say
*down at the top, come on, down at the top, up from the
bottom* or, lock the back door, *cierra la puerta de atrás.*

Burge What's that?

Nina Lock the back door.

Burge Is it significant, do you think, he says that in
Spanish?

Nina No.

Int: **Nina's** *flat. Bathroom. Night.*

Nina *finishes brushing her teeth. She rinses the brush and
returns it to the glass.*

Jamie (*OOV*) *Cierra la puerta de atrás.*

Nina (*smiles*) I did. It's locked.

Burge (*VO*) How long ago did Jamie die?

Nina *wipes her mouth with a flannel.*

Burge (*VO*) Nina?

Nina *pulls the cord and plunges the room into black.*

And on the black screen we get –

Burge (*VO over credits*) Jamie, when was it he died?

*Music is playing. Bach's Sonata No 3 for Cello (Viol de
gamba) and Piano, 2nd Movement.*

The cello is supple, straining with emotion.

We're still on black, but the camera is moving and finds, in black and white, a cello in close, hands coaxing the strings. It's **Jamie.**

He plays and we see him full length, bent over his instrument intent. Pull out and then freeze the image.

Int: **Nina**'s *living room. Morning.*

Keep pulling out and find that the image is now a photograph inside a frame and that the photograph is in **Nina**'s *bedroom.*

As the image freezes to become this photograph, the cello line is replaced by a voice, humming.

The camera tracks across the bedroom, across the hall, past the bathroom and kitchen to discover **Nina** *playing the piano.*

By the piano, a cello leans against the wall. She half sings the cello part. This is clearly something of a ritual for her.

The flat is tasteful, not without humour, untidy, evidence of a chaotic life. The Latin American countries make a significant cultural contribution.

There is a work area, a table loaded with files and papers, a pinboard with some industrial instruction sheets, a couple of record sleeves.

Nina *closes her eyes as she vocalises the cello part. Something makes her open them. She stops playing, freezes. Her eyes go glassy.*

A rat scampers across the top of the piano. Obviously a Bach fan.

Nina *regards it calmly for a second or two. Then she gasps and stares at the rat.*

Int: Translation agency. Day.

A kind of neighbourhood translation supermarket, where you can get walk-in advice and translations in twenty-eight languages in a small scruffy open-plan office. It's the end of the day and the office is closing.

Sandy *is boss.*

Nina *works at a computer on her desk. The* **Translator** *prepares to go.*

Translator   N'night, bye.

Nina   Are you off, Carolyn? 'Bye.

Translator   Yeah. See you tomorrow.

Nina   N'night.

Translator   Night, Sandy.

Sandy   Oh, 'bye Carolyn. 'Bye.

Nina *goes back to the screen.* **Sandy** *is ready to go. He comes over. He is a lovable, maudlin Scot whose life is a disaster.*

Sandy   I like your hair.

Nina   What?

Sandy   Your hair, it looks, is it different? Or is it the earrings? They're terrific. They look, sort of, are they sort of Inca?

Nina   Sandy – what are you talking about?

Sandy   Are you depressed?

Nina   No.

Sandy   I don't just love you because you translate my postcards, you know.

Nina   I know.

Sandy   You see everybody's just a wee bit concerned about you.

Nina Everybody who?

Sandy 'Cause you've disappeared. You've gone to ground. You don't come out to play anymore. You don't invite people round, you look terrible.

Nina Except for my hair.

Sandy Actually, Nina, your hair – well, your hair was never your strong point. Is it still Jamie?

Nina (*thrown*) What?

Sandy I can understand that. Lord knows I miss Gabriella and I hated her and I still miss her but you know I can understand that. You know – you've got to get out – unless you get out, you'll never meet anybody.

Nina Okay. Okay, darling. Thanks. Thanks.

They hug.

Sandy So, come on, come on, have a wee drink with your Uncle Sandy.

Nina *goes to the door.*

Nina (*distressed*) Sandy, I can't. I can't. I just can't.

Int: **Nina**'s *flat. Hall and living room. Night.*

Nina *goes to the elaborate collection of locks and bolts at her front door.* **Titus**, *her carpenter friend, is outside.*

Nina (*opening the door*) Hi. (*At the lateness of the visit.*) Everything okay?

Titus *is Polish and earnest. He examines the locks and bolts.*

Titus Good. Very safe now.

Nina Oh, yes – I'm really much happier with the door.

Titus Take ten men to break down this door.

Nina   Titus, it's nearly midnight.

Titus   Yes, I come to see if you still want me in the morning.

Nina   Oh yes, I do, actually please. Yeah, I can't close any of my kitchen cabin – oh and, Titus listen I've got rats, I've either got two massive rats who never stop eating, or about two thousand with normal, who are on a calorie controlled diet.

She wanders through into the living room, from which it's possible to see the kitchen area.

Nina   I had this man come this morning and he put down poison, he said it was enough to knock out half of North London, and it's disappearing. Look.

She picks up one of the foil containers and shows it to him.

Titus   I'm missing Poland.

Nina   Right.

Titus   Sometimes I think I hate Poland, but then a song goes through my head, some music, or the taste, I remember taste of Polish bread of (*shrugs.*) a man should never drink. He remembers only his country, his mother, his lovers.

Nina   Yeah. I'm going to bed. I'm bushed. I've had a – it's been a really busy day.

Titus   You are the only beautiful woman I meet in London.

Nina   Absolutely right. That's got nothing to do with the drink. I am the only beautiful woman in London. Ni-night. See you in the morning.

Titus   In my country when we want to be rid of rats we do not use poison – we dance. To drive the rats away we – we dance.

And **Titus** *begins to dance, heavy, drunk, splendid,*

*romantic. Involves many solemn claps. The music is
'Bleeding Heart' — traditional.*

Nina *sinks onto the floor. But she enjoys the performance.*
Titus *takes his coat.*

Titus   I would be surprised if the rats will come back.

Int: **Nina**'s *bedroom. Night.*

Nina *is in bed. A rat toddles up the bed along the duvet,
perilously close to* **Nina**'s *head.*

Nina *is disturbed by the sound. Her eyes flash wide. In the
darkness.*

Nina (*quietly*)   Oh my *God*.

Int: **Nina**'s *living room. Morning.*

Nina *is wrapped in the duvet in the living room. She slept
on the sofa. She embraces a cricket bat. She's fast asleep.
She's had a difficult night.*

Int: **Nina**'s *bathroom. Morning.*

Nina *looks at the tray of rat poison. She examines herself
in the mirror. Is not impressed.*

*She bends over the bath, puts the mat on the floor, and
opens the hot tap. Nothing happens. She tries the cold tap.
Steaming brown water trickles through, accompanied by a
loud knocking sound.*

Ext. **Nina**'s *street and flat. Morning.*

Sandy *cycles along the street up to* **Nina**'s *building. He
dismounts and props his bicycle up inside the gate.*

He stumbles up the front steps.

Int: **Nina**'*s hall. Morning.*

All the floorboards in the hall are up. The front door is open.

A **Plumber** *is under the floorboards.*

Sandy *comes through the door. He's carrying some files and material for translation.*

He steps apologetically over the **Plumber**.

Sandy Sorry. Sorry. Is Nina around?

Plumber Through there.

Sandy Thanks.

Int: **Nina**'*s living room. Morning.*

Nina, *dressed, is at the table eating borshch.*

Titus *has practically dismantled the kitchen and is working away, hammer, saw and sawdust.*

Sandy *is confused.*

Sandy Nina?

Nina (*pleased*) Sandy.

Sandy What's going on?

Nina Well, the fridge is still working. That's what I keep telling myself. The fish fingers are frozen.

Sandy (*sympathetically*) Oh, Nina, this flat, it's not been very, really, has it? Who's the chappie in the joists?

Nina He's the plumber, little problem with the water. Apart from anything else it's gone brown. Titus is trying to make the kitchen doors fit the cabinets, you've met Titus? – Titus, this is Sandy – Sandy runs the agency.

Titus *nods*.

Sandy Hello, Titus.

Titus Hello.

Sandy Good work.

Nina And George is here somewhere. George? No, the whole place is falling to bits. It's a disaster. Why did I buy it, Sandy? You told me, Jamie told me, everybody told me.

George *appearing, holding the foil trays*.

George Nina, this is very important. (*Sees* **Sandy**.) Hello.

Nina George, this is Sandy. He's my boss.

Sandy Hello, George.

George Have you touched these containers?

Nina No.

George You haven't emptied them out or. . . ?

Nina No.

George (*in a continuous breath*) We've got a very serious problem here, Nina, we're talking a lot of rodents, we're talking infestation, we may even be talking nesting. Could I make a telephone call?

Nina Sure.

Sandy What's this, mice?

Nina No, no. (*She indicates the size of these creatures.*)

Sandy Rats?! Oh, my God.

Nina I have to move out.

Titus Sandy, you want Borshch?

Nina Have some. Titus says it's the answer to all our problems.

Sandy (*accepting the Borshch*) Borshch? Thanks. Nina, I've had a little postcard from Charlie. Can you spare a few minutes?

Nina Sandy, you've got to learn Spanish.

Sandy I know.

Nina It's so perverse to run a language agency, speak, how many languages do you speak? but not – I mean it's your son, you've got to understand what he's telling you . . .

Sandy I know.

Nina I mean, in the end, that was the problem with you and Gabriella, you couldn't say anything to each other.

Sandy (*solemn*) No, no, that was its strength. It was when we started to communicate it went wrong. Before that it was terrific. Sign language. It was great. Voilà.

Nina You're a twerp.

There's a whole pile of stuff besides the postcard.

Nina What's all this?

Sandy *prodding it perfunctorily.*

Sandy Work, it's urgent, it's stuff, it's urgent so I brought it with me, it's some manuals and, whatever, but the postcard, can you just sightread the postcard, Nina, because I'm beginning to have an anxiety attack.

Nina (*reading*) 'Dear Daddy . . .'

Sandy Where does it say that?

Nina *Querido papà*. There.

Sandy Fantastic.

Nina 'Dear Daddy, we are spending our holiday in Mar del Plata' . . . lovely, supposed to be beautiful . . .

'I am swimming in the sea and do not, I'm not wearing . . .' uh, what's the name of those, 'I'm not wearing . . .'

Sandy Trunks?

Nina Things, floats. 'Mario is teaching me to swim underwater.'

Sandy Bastard.

Nina 'We're staying in a big hotel which has a television in the bathroom.'

Sandy Oh – that's the thing with Gabriella, give her a television in the bathroom, doesn't that make you laugh, doesn't that make you spew after all that stuff about materialism, a television in the bathroom!

Nina (*ploughing on*) 'Last night we went to see a football match and had a barbecue which gave me diarrhoea.'

Sandy That is terrible. Because Mario, who's a bastard, that's beyond dispute, he's absolutely and manifestly a bastard, is in loco parentis, is he not? Instead he's poisoning my son.

Nina 'I'm having a great time. Wish you were here. Lots of love, Charlie.'

Sandy *after a pause, bleak.*

Sandy Yeah. Yeah. Yeah.

Nina (*nicely*) He's having a great time.

Sandy I have to write back. Nina, would you help me write back?

Nina (*exasperated*) If you promise me you'll make an effort to learn Spanish.

Sandy Si, si. Thank you. You're a good person.

Sandy *hugs* **Nina**.

Titus *leans over the kitchen balcony, wielding a hammer.*

Titus How is soup? Fantastic?

Nina It's fantastic.

Sandy Fantasic.

Titus *ladling some more food onto their plates.*

Titus I tell her last night Nina she is beautiful woman.

Sandy She is beautiful. You are.

Nina (*embarrassed*) Okay.

George *reappears.*

George I think she's beautiful.

Plumber Who's this who's beautiful?

George We're talking about Nina.

Plumber Yeah, she is.

Nina (*embarrassed*) Guys. What is this.

Ext: Walled garden. Morning.

Nina *is taking her laundry into the tiny garden area.*

Int: Kitchen area. Morning.

The four men, **Titus, Sandy, George** *and the* **Plumber** *are doing the washing up.*

They survey **Nina** *benevolently as she pegs out her washing.*

Sandy (*washing*) She really loved him, tragic. And, you know, he was young, he was younger than me, so, it was really cruel, harsh. One minute he had a sore throat, next minute he's having an examination, next minute he's stopped breathing. The anaesthetist couldn't get the tube down. If he'd had a wee suck at a Strepsil it would never have happened.

Titus (*drying*) I think she loves me. I think now she does not know yet, but . . .

Titus *makes a gesture of blossoming.*

Plumber (*also drying*) Do you like washing?

Sandy Yes. I love getting my hands in warm water.

Plumber I like drying.

Titus Also me.

George Me too.

Sandy Look at this water. It's brown.

Plumber It's a miracle there's any water.

Sandy This is a terrible flat.

Ext: **Nina**'s *walled garden. Morning.*

Outside **Nina** *pegs up her clothes. As she pegs her wet shirt to the line it obliterates her vision.*

The breeze fills the shirt, puffing out the arms.

Nina (*VO*) . . . or I find that I've just been sitting with my head in my hands and an hour has gone by, or longer, like this (*demonstrating*) – with the heel of my palm pressed into my eyes and I'm completely numb –

Int: **Burge**, *the therapist. Morning.*

Nina *sits in the chair by a window. The sky outside is visible.*

Nina – and the kettle can be boiling away, or the telephone, um – and I'm crying, I'm crying. I mean I can be on the tube and somebody says what's the matter? and there are tears, it's ridiculous. I miss him. I

just miss him. I miss him. I miss him. I know I
shouldn't do this.

*She's weeping. It starts as tears dissociated from her tone
of voice and gradually takes over, making it impossible for
her to continue.*

Nina   I'm in the sitting room and I think there's no
point going to bed, he's not there, or I'm in bed, I
think there's no point getting up, it's anger, isn't it, it's
rage, it's rage. I get so angry with people, other people,
other people in love, or out of love, or wasting love, and
women with children, growing children, fertile, but
most of all I'm angry with him. I'm so angry with him.
I can't forgive him for not being here. I can't – (*And
she can't continue.*) Oh God.

Burge *lets her weep.* **Nina** *weeps and weeps. It goes on
and on.*

Burge *sits in silence.* **Burge** *switches off the tape
recorder. Says nothing.*

Nina, *snapping out of her mood.*

Nina   Oh God. I've run over, haven't I? I'm sorry.
Sorry. I'm fine, actually. I am fine. Oh God, I'm late.
Listen, I'll see you next Tuesday. Thanks.

Takes a tissue from **Burge**'*s box, checking for permission.*

Nina   Can I?

She blows her nose and starts to go.

Nina   Bye.

Ext: Park. Morning.

Nina *walks with* **Maura**. *English lessons.*

Maura   We walk.

Nina   We do walk. Yeah.

Maura   We looking at things.

Nina (*correcting*) *Are* looking.

Maura   Yes.

Nina   Say it. (*For* **Maura** *to repeat.*) We are looking at things.

Maura   We are looking at things.

Nina   So, what things can we see?

Maura   Ah, we can see – trees.

Nina   Good, we can see trees.

Maura   Yeah, uh, people.

Nina   Good. We can see some people.

Maura   And, we can see some people. Can see cielo – ah cielo. Uh, no me lo digas.

Nina   Ss – sky.

Maura   Sky, sky.

Nina   Very good.

Maura   We can see the sky and the . . . nubes – i nubes!

Nina (*translating*)   Clouds.

Maura (*trying*)   Clowed.

Nina (*carefully*)   Clouds.

Maura (*better*)   Cloudds, yeah.

Nina   Yeh. (*Looking.*) Yeah, that's right, Maura, we can see the clouds in the sky.

They look up at the sky. Exquisite, delicate clouds.

Int: **Nina**'s *kitchen/living room. Day.*

Nina *is in the kitchen. Her nephew,* **Harry,** *eleven, sits on the fridge.*

Nina *puts her fingers to her lips, opens a Mars bar, stuffs it in* **Harry's** *mouth. He grins.*

The sound of the vacuum cleaner distracts **Nina**. *It's* **Claire**, *her sister and friend.*

Nina   What are you doing?

Nina *goes down into the living room.*

Claire   It's no problem. We can gossip while we're cleaning.

Nina   Claire, I've had plumbers – who're coming back, carpenters, rat catchers and apparently now there's subsidence in one of the supporting walls . . . being house proud gets a touch difficult.

Claire   Well, vacuuming won't hurt. Leave me alone. I like cleaning.

Nina   You're just like Ma.

Claire   I am not. Shut up. You've always liked messing. I've always liked cleaning. I wish you'd let me help you more, I could always pop round and –

Nina *goes back to the kitchen.*

Nina   No thanks.

Claire   Harry, what're you doing?

Harry *is putting his hand into a tray of rat poison.*

Nina (*dashing across*)   That's rat poison! Harry! Harry, that's poison!

Claire *dashing across, the unattended Hoover, going berserk.*

Claire   God!

Harry, *looking a little sheepish.*

Claire   Did you eat any of this stuff, oh God, did you?

Harry *shakes his head.*

Claire   What's that in your mouth? Spit it out! Spit it out!

Claire *rinses* **Harry**'s *mouth.*

Nina   That's chocolate, the poison's purple. (*Stabs at her own chest.*) My fault.

Claire (*admonishing*)   Sit down. Just sit down for God's sake, and try not to – He's impossible!

Nina *leans over the balcony and kisses* **Harry**'s *head.*

Nina   But you love him.

Claire   I love him, but he's impossible. I don't always love him. Just try not to poison yourself for five minutes.

They all sit down, after **Claire** *has wrestled with the Hoover.*

Oh Nina, how can you have rats?

Nina   It's a personality defect.

Claire   I'm serious.

Nina   I haven't spoken to them, Claire. I tried, but they won't answer. 'What are you doing here?' Nothing. It's the poison. They're sulking.

Claire   There's an odour. I have to say. There's a strong odour. Even Harry noticed.

Nina (*exasperated*)   Well the rats are dying, Claire. That's basically the problem on the smell front.

Claire   I wish you'd come and stay with us. You could have people in and have it all done properly, or sell it. I can't bear to think of you living here all on your own.

Nina   I'm fine.

Claire   It's not as if Jamie ever lived here.

Nina   It's got nothing to do with Jamie. Honestly, darling. Thank you, but I'm fine. You know if I came and lived with you, we'd drive each other bonkers, I mean, anyway where would I actually stay?

Claire   It is a small house. It's the kids. I say all that but I, sometimes I wish I could escape somewhere myself. No, you're right, it's a stupid idea. I'll come and live here, and the men can all . . . what do you think?

Nina   How's Nick?

Claire   Yes. He's busy. Do you know about Everest?

Harry   Dad's going to climb Mount Everest.

Nina   You're joking . . . when?

Claire   Well, after Christmas sometime.

Nina   When's the baby due?

Claire (*defensive*)   Oh no, no, the baby'll be two or three months by then. It's fine. It's fine. He probably won't go. He's hopeless with babies anyway, so I –

Nina   I can't sell the flat. Nobody's buying even nice flats. Only a lunatic would, anyway I like it. I like it.

Nina *comes to sit on the sofa beside* **Claire**.

Harry *has come over and arranged himself on* **Nina**'s *lap*.

Harry (*nicely*)   I like it.

Nina   Exactly. Harry likes it.

Harry   It's big.

Nina   Oh – so are you. (*To* **Harry**.) What's the verdict on a new baby?

Harry   I don't mind.

Nina   You're looking fab. How's school?

Claire   He's worried because he doesn't think there'll be room in our bed for four.

Nina (*squeezing him*)   'Course there is. Shove, that's the secret. Tactical use of the elbow.

Claire He's doing brilliantly at school. He loves it.

Nina (*frowning*) You're not getting posh.

Harry No.

Nina Good. Say bum and Trotsky twice a day before meals.

Claire Harry, don't. Have you told Nina about your lessons? He's having cello lessons.

Nina (*suddenly tight*) Oh, really?

Claire Isn't that great? (*To* **Harry**.) Are you going to ask Nina?

Harry (*shy*) You ask her.

Nina What's this?

Claire Well, Harry was wondering, he's having these lessons and, at some point – well, the school provides boys with an instrument – until you sort of decide whether or not it's serious, whether or not the boy is going to persevere . . . but then, obviously he'll need his own cello.

Nina Yeah – so what are you getting at?

Claire Well, obviously say if this is a bad idea, but we did wonder, we were wondering whether Jamie's cello, is that a terrible idea? You don't play it and perhaps . . .

Nina *in an almost unrecognisable tone.*

Nina You want me to give you Jamie's cello?

Claire No, not give, no. No. Um. I mean either for Harry to borrow it or we'll try and buy it or –

Nina Have you any idea how much that cello is worth?

Claire Well I know it's a good one, of course –

Nina (*distraught*) I can't believe you'd be so

insensitive. That's practically all I've got of him. It is him. It is him. It's like asking me to give you his body.

Claire (*over this*)   – Oh Nina, it isn't –

Nina (*ploughing on*)   Well, anyway, you can't have it.

Claire   Okay. I'm sorry. I'm sorry. You're right it was . . .

Nina (*losing her grip*)   You should never have asked. It's so horrible.

Claire   I had no idea you'd react so . . . Nina . . . Nina . . .

Nina *is closing right down. Paralysed.*

Int: **Nina**'s *living room. Night.*

Nina *sits on the floor, holding the cello in her arms. She puts it on the floor, and goes to the piano. She plays the Bach duet.*

The cello part comes in, sweet, intense, moving.

Nina *comes to terms with the fact that there does really seem to be a cello playing in the room. She does not, dare not, turn round.*

But then the cello stops. Her face falls. She lets out a sharp sigh and stops playing herself. She leans forward and puts her head in her hands.

Jamie *is there, tangible, loving her, pulling her up, embracing her, and she cries and laughs and cries and can't believe what's happening.*

Int: **Nina**'s *kitchen. Night.*

Jamie *and* **Nina** *sit on the kitchen floor, cuddled up together.*

Jamie I kept thinking – just my luck – die of a sore throat.

Nina But dying, actually dying – what's it like?

Jamie Dying's okay. It was the general anaesthetic I didn't like.

Nina I'm serious.

Jamie So am I. I don't know, maybe I didn't die properly, maybe that's why I can come back . . . It was like walking behind a glass wall while everybody else got on with missing me. It didn't hurt. You know I'm very sensitive to pain.

Nina Um.

Jamie It really didn't hurt.

Nina But where do you go? I mean, do you go to Heaven, or what?

Jamie I don't think so.

Nina I can't take all this in. Where do I start? Are you here? You are here?

Jamie I am here.

Nina Are you staying?

Jamie Well, I think so. I'd like to. Is that all right?

Nina It's fantastic. Can I kiss you?

Jamie Yeah.

They kiss.

Nina Your lips are a bit cold.

Jamie Actually, I'm fantastically cold. That's one thing I've really noticed. This flat is freezing.

Nina Well, the heating's on. It's supposed to be on, anyway.

Jamie I've gotta tell you – this is a terrible flat.

Nina   I know.

Jamie   It's terrible. Honestly, Nina, you're hopeless. And something else is really bothering me too. You've got red bills. Red gas, red phone . . . it's not clever.

Nina   I know. I know.

Jamie   And you never lock the back door. It's driving me crazy.

Nina   I'm going. I'm going.

And she does, unravelling herself from him.

Ext. **Nina**'s *walled garden. Night.*

Nina *is fiddling outside, bringing in washing.*

Jamie *appears in the doorway. Watches her.*

Jamie (*soft now*)   Thank you for missing me.

Nina   I have. I do. I did.

Jamie   I know. But the pain, your pain, I couldn't bear that. There's a little girl, I see this little girl from time to time, Alice, who's three, three and a half, and she's great, everybody loves her, makes a big fuss, but she's not spoiled, well she wasn't spoiled, and she was knocked over, and her parents, and her family, the friends from kindergarten – she used to go to this park – and she was telling me, she, they made an area in the park, gave the money for swings and little wooden animals, and there are these plaques on each of the, on the sides of the swing, the bottom of the horse. 'From Alice's Mum and Dad. In loving memory of Alice who used to play here.' And, of course, Alice goes back there all the time. You see parents take their child off the swing and see the sign and then they hold on to their son and daughter so tightly, clinging on for dear life, and yet the capacity to love, people have, what happens to it?

Nina   I don't know.

Jamie (*wry*)   I blame the government.

Nina   What?

Jamie   The government.

Nina   What's the government got to do with anything?

Jamie   I hate the bastards.

Nina (*incredulous*)   You've died and you're still into party politics?

Jamie (*proudly*)   I still attend meetings.

Nina   Oh God.

Jamie (*pointedly*)   Which is more than can be said for some other people.

The doorbell rings.

Nina   That's my doorbell.

Jamie   It's a bit late. You expecting somebody?

Nina   Uh no.

Jamie   Oh – I'll make myself scarce.

Int: **Nina**'*s front door. Night.*

Nina *opens the door to discover* **Titus.**

Titus   I make decision. We go to Paris. Make love for one week.

Nina   Titus.

She starts to laugh. It's not cruel. It's a nice, helpless laugh. She's very touched.

Nina   You're fab. You're so sweet.

Titus *smiles, hands her a plane ticket.*

Nina   Oh Titus, I can't go to Paris with you. (*At the ticket.*) Oh dear.

Titus Why? You – you don't like Paris? You don't want to make love?

Nina (*teasing*) For a week? (*Then gently.*) No, no, no, no, I love Paris. No, it's got nothing to do with your offer which is very kind, no, which is more than kind, it's lovely. It's just that I'm not really looking for a lover, to be . . . It's not you. I'd say the same to anybody.

Titus Can I come in?

Nina No.

Titus Just for talk.

Nina No, really. It's too late.

Titus Now I am depressed.

Nina I'm sorry.

Titus I bought tickets. I am man with big emotion, big heart.

Nina I know, Titus. Thank you.

Titus (*resigned now*) Well. I love you. You follow.

Nina I follow.

Nina *closes the door.*

Int: **Nina's** *flat. Hall to living room. Night.*

Nina *comes down the hall.* **Jamie** *appears to have disappeared. She explores the living room and kitchen.*

Nina Jamie?

She looks more carefully.

Nina Jamie?

She's suddenly desperate.

Nina Jamie, please, where are you?

Int: Landing outside **Nina's** *flat. Night.*

From where he crouches, outside **Nina's** *door,* **Titus** *hears this plaintive call.*

Nina (*OOV*)   Jamie? Please, come back.

Titus *listens, frowns.*

Int: **Nina's** *bedroom. Night.*

Nina *sits on her bed, her hand over her eyes.*

Jamie (*casually*)   Who was that?

And he's sitting beside her on the bed. **Nina** *screams.*

Nina (*exasperated*)   Is this going to be your party trick?

Jamie   Sounded like a man's voice.

Nina   Titus. It was Titus. Don't worry. (*As an afterthought.*) He's Polish.

Jamie   Bit late to come round.

Nina   That's what I told him.

Jamie   So, what – is he in love with you?

Nina   I don't think so, no.

Jamie *blows into his hands, presses his palms to his lips.*

Nina   Darling? What are you doing?

Jamie   Warming my lips.

And they kiss in the half light.

Int: **Nina's** *living room. Morning.*

Nina *and* **Jamie** *look out of the large window at the back of the house. They are playing the cloud game.*

They kneel on the sofa. **Nina**, *as they characterise the clouds.*

Nina   Australia!

Jamie   Where?

Nina (*pointing*)   There.

Jamie   Good. (*Scours.*) Two lovers!

Nina   Where?

Jamie (*pointing*)   There. No arms, losing their legs, and . . . actually . . . becoming Europe.

Nina   I can't see Europe.

Jamie   Europe without Italy or Spain.

Nina   That's hardly Europe. (*Of another.*) Your mother!

Jamie   You think every cloud looks like my mother.

Nina   This really does look like your mother. Look! Eyes, nose, the eyebrows, it's brilliant!

Jamie   My mother has not got a beard.

Nina   I see that as a sort of a – um ruffle.

They stare. They watch the clouds.

Nina *sings absently – snatches from Joni Mitchell's 'A Case of You'.*

Now **Jamie** *is joining in. They're hardly aware of singing.*

Then smiling, acknowledging the duet.

Nina   I love you.

Jamie   I love you.

Nina   I really love you.

Jamie   I really truly love you.

Nina   I really truly madly love you.

Jamie   I really truly madly deeply love you.

Nina   I really truly madly deeply passionately love you.

Jamie   I really truly madly deeply passionately remarkably love you.

Nina   Remarkably? Okay: I really truly madly deeply passionately remarkably deliciously love you.

Jamie   I really truly madly passionately remarkably deliciously juicily love you.

Nina (*pouncing*)   Deeply! Deeply! You passed on deeply! Which was your word, which means that you couldn't have meant it. You're a fraud. You're probably a figment of my imagination. And juicily!! Your forfeit. You play, I dance!

Nina *jumps off the sofa and dashes out of the living room.*

Jamie *closes the windows and looks at the clouds.*

Int: **Nina**'s *living room. Morning.*

Nina *danced, naked under* **Jamie**'s *coat.*

Jamie *plays a cello version of The Walker Brothers' 'The Sun Ain't Gonna Shine Anymore'.*

Very solemn. Both of them singing. He sings the words, she sings 'Jamie baby' at intervals.

Nina *goes to the piano to play the chorus.* **Jamie** *puts down his cello and jumps over the settee to join* **Nina** *at the piano. They sing the chorus together.*

The doorbell rings. They duck down under the piano.

Jamie   I'll go.

He means he'll disappear.

Nina   No. No.

They crawl to the window. **Nina** *looks out. It's* **Claire** *carrying a peace offering, a huge plant.*

Nina   Oh, it's Claire.

Jamie   She wanted my cello, didn't she? Bloody cheek!

Nina   I want the world to go away.

Jamie   Well, I don't know about the world, but I guarantee the rats have gone away.

Nina   How?

Jamie   Terrified of ghosts.

Nina   Really?

Jamie   Really. (*Looking out of the window.*) And now your sister's gone away too.

Claire *and* **Harry** *are going out of the front gate.*

Int: **Nina**'s *bedroom. Morning.*

Nina's *asleep.* **Jamie** *watching her.*

He's wearing his overcoat. He goes over to the bed, kneels down onto it, and begins, quirkily, to wake **Nina**. *He sings into her ear, jiving a little.*

Jamie *sings, in passing imitation of Bob Dylan, from 'Tangled Up In Blue'.*

He's nuzzling her, she's trying to hide under a pillow.

Nina   Ngggh. Go away.

Now it's Buddy Holly.

Jamie *sings from 'Raining In My Heart'.*

Jamie *picks up a glass and drips water onto* **Nina**.

Nina   Oh God. I'm ill.

Jamie   You're not ill.

Nina   I'm sick.

Jamie   You're not sick.

Nina   I am sick, I've got tummy ache, I'm probably dying too. That'll be the next thing – I'll die as well.

Jamie *doesn't immediately respond.* **Nina***'s head pokes up from under the pillow.*

Nina   Oh, sorry, sorry that was, I can't believe I said that.

Jamie   I was wondering whether you were going to work today.

Nina   No.

Jamie   Okay.

Nina (*of dying*)   I can't believe I just said that.

Jamie   Don't worry.

The telephone rings. After four rings, the answer machine engages.

Jamie (*wry*)   You should call in, so they know you're dying. They might be concerned.

Sandy (*on answer phone*)   Nina. This is Sandy. Are you hibernating? Where are you?

Nina   Do you think I should go in? Aren't you boiling?

Jamie   I'm frozen, I've been trying to fix your central heating. Who put it in? It's unbelievable, what was wrong with thing, the guy, what was his name who did the shower at Coniston Road?

Nina   It's working perfectly, it must be ninety degrees in here. Probably why I've got stomach ache. It's probably some tropical disease. I've probably got cholera, malaria! I can't go into work with malaria. Anyway . . . what would you do if I went to work?

Jamie   Me? Don't worry about me, it's a time to catch up with a lot of things, I've been having Spanish lessons, I've been reading some very long . . .

Nina (*cutting in*) Spanish! I knew! I knew you had!

Jamie Oh?

Nina Because you were always, when I sensed you around, when I could sense you and feel you, and you were speaking, telling me to lock the back door you'd say, you'd say it in Spanish. And I was so, I was really, I was really touched that you . . . (*Can't resist.*) The accent's not great. But –

Jamie *drags* **Nina** *off the bed and pushes her towards the living room.*

She wanders through, looks at the number of messages on the machine, frowns, then stumbles into the living room. Something has been changed.

Nina So I'm going in, am I? Oh, Jamie. what have you – what have –

Jamie *comes through.*

Jamie I changed a few things around. Tidied up a bit.

Nina (*interrupting*) Where's my tiger?

Jamie Better isn't it? (*Inquiring.*) I can change it back.

Nina No. No.

Jamie (*light*) You know I've got more sense of those things, you could never hang a picture, or – you know – could I light the fire?

Jamie *holes up a cloud mobile, which is tangled.*

Jamie I gave you this.

Nina I think I will have to go in, actually I can feel my face is hot.

Jamie Well, I've gotta be careful. Because you know I'm prone to colds, and, you imagine, I get a cold now it could last for ever.

Nina *laughs.* **Jamie** *doesn't.*

Jamie I'm not joking. I'm serious.

She looks at him. Considers.

Nina   Thank you. (*Suddenly moved.*)

Jamie   What for?

Nina   Coming back.

Int: Translation office. Day.

It's a little like Babel as Chinese, Czech, French, Punjabi, Turkish, Greek, Italian leak from desk to desk.

People are here for immigration advice, for industrial translations, for medical interpretation, for help with letters to MPs, Local Authority communication, etc.

Members of staff work at terminals, doing postal translations or speak strange tongues into telephones. Exotic dictionaries abound.

Sandy *has a client who has bought a video machine and can't follow the instructions.*

Maura, *heavily pregnant, is carrying a black plastic bag across the room.*

Nina *comes in, rather furtively, carrying various items of translation work. Yellow stickers on the desk.*

Sandy *looks up from where he works.*

Nina (*to* **Translator**)   Hi.

Sandy   Nina!

Nina   I'm sorry, I'm sorry, I'm sorry, I'm sorry, I'm sorry. (*She spots* **Maura**.) Maura, hello! Oh my God, is it Thursday?

Sandy   It's Friday, Nina. Where've you been?

Titus *comes into the office, carrying a plank.*

Nina   Titus, hello.

Titus (*straight-faced*)   Hello.

Nina   Maura, has she been, have you been here since yesterday? ¿Has estado aquí desde ayer?

Maura   No, no.

Sandy   She's doing some cleaning.

Nina   What do you mean?

Sandy   She's cleaning. We need someone, and she needs the money.

Nina   Sandy, she's about to have a baby.

Sandy   Excuse me, excuse me, could we just start all this again, please! You've disappeared off the face of the planet for a week, we have been working. You come back, we get told off.

To his French client, in English.

Sandy   Sorry about this.

Frenchman   Comment?

Sandy (*English*)   I'll be with you in a minute.

Frenchman   Comment?

Nina   God, is it really Friday? My God.

Sandy   Apart from anything else, Gabriella called me, and she was screaming and yelling and being hysterical, what else is new I know, but lucky for me Maura was here . . .

Nina   How did that help?

Sandy   Gabriella spoke to her, now Maura can speak to you . . . then you can speak to me.

Nina (*perplexed*)   Oh, and what about Titus? Do we get all the ex-clients to come and work here now?

Sandy   Excuse me.

Frenchman *anxious about the time.*

Frenchman   Monsieur!

Sandy *without pausing for breath, but switching into French.*

Sandy Je sais, je sais. Vous devez prendre l'avion. (*Back to* **Nina** *and English.*) Well – what about an explanation, make something up . . . and why've you got the nerve to look so cheerful?

Nina That's a really tricky one, Sandy.

Sandy Yeah, I thought it might be.

Nina Do you love me?

Sandy No.

Nina No, I mean as a friend?

Sandy No.

Nina You do love me as a friend!

Sandy No, I don't.

Frenchman Je vous en prie, je dois aller à l'aeroport.

Sandy (*in French, hugely irritable*) Pourquoi vous n'avez pas acheter cet appareil en France?

Frenchman Je le demande.

Sandy (*to* **Nina**) And you'd better ring Rachel Reed . . .

Nina (*this is an interesting name for her*) Oh. Did she say what it was?

Sandy And I hope you're too late 'cause she rang on Monday. (*Straight back to the video manual*) Maintenant. Monsieur. (*Reads.*) The fourteen day timer . . . (*Translates to French.*) La bouton programmation de quatorze jours.

Nina Sandy, I can tell you're forgiving me.

Sandy *doesn't pause, but glares affectionately at her. During this* **Titus** *walks by* **Nina**'s *desk on the way to the back of the office.*

Nina   Are you okay?

Titus *shrugs miserably.*

Titus   I come tonight, finish your cabinets?

Nina   Well, tonight's not a good, it's not a . . .

Titus   Okay, I come tomorrow.

Nina (*evasive*)   Well, can we, can we talk about that tomorrow, can I telephone you?

Titus   Sure.

Nina   It's not that I don't want you to come and finish the, it's I've got some people staying at the moment, friends, and, they turned up unexpectedly, and –

Titus   Okay.

He continues on his journey. With a heavy heart.

Nina *sits at her desk, moves the deluge of paper about for a few seconds. Sighs. The languages flow around her head.*

Titus *helps* **Maura** *carry a dustbin bag across the office.*

Ext: The park. Day.

Maura *and* **Nina** *walking. We see their reflection in the water.*

Nina   How's the baby?

Maura   Good. Very fine.

Nina   Very fine's not, we don't say very fine, but I like it.

Maura   How should I say?

Nina   Very fine's fine.

Maura   Tus amigos, Sandy y los otros, están muy preocupados por tí.

They walk up the steps.

Nina   English, Maura.

Maura   Oh, I can't.

Nina   Yes, you can.

Maura   Erm, Sandy, er, Titus, eh, very sad for you.

Nina   Why are they sad for me?

Maura   Because her man is dead.

Nina   Your man. My man. Yes, well.

Maura   I also sad.

Nina   Maura, do you believe in life after death?

Maura *frowns, she doesn't understand.*

Nina   ¿La vida después de la muerte, espíritus?

Maura   ¿Espíritus? Sí, claro.

They walk along an arched walkway.

Maura   Yo hice una película, un documentál en Chile, sobre fantasmas y – ¡claro que creo!

Nina   You made a documentary?

Maura   Sí, yo hago películas.

Nina   Oh English, English.

Maura   I make film. Many film. In Chile. In Chile I make film. In London I am cleaner. Ach!

She smiles. **Nina** *puts an arm through hers. They walk.*

Maura   The spirits are everywhere. They are walking here with us.

Nina   Oh yes.

They pass a tombstone with a statue of an angel on its side.

Int: Cafe in the park. Day.

Nina *and* **Maura** *come into the cafe. It's quiet. The odd pigeon from the park pecking at the entrance.*

Only one or two of the tables are occupied, mostly elderly Highgate intellectuals, but at one table, a youngish man sits, half-eating, half-absorbed, in a novel.

Maura *knows several of the waiters and waitresses who work at this cafe, including* **Roberto**. *She greets* **Roberto** *and they find a table.*

Roberto   Hola Maura.

Maura (*to* **Nina** *as they sit down*)   I was working here before.

Nina   Oh did you? It's lovely.

Roberto *has come across, he embraces* **Maura**.

Roberto   ¿Como estás?

Maura   Bien, bien. Roberto, this is my friend, Nina. Nina, this is Roberto.

Nina   Hello.

Roberto (*very warm, shaking her hand*)   I am very pleased to meet you. Maura told us you help her.

Nina   Oh, well.

Roberto (*to* **Maura**)   Esperame un momento que yo regreso. ¿Café?

Maura   Mm, café, sí.

Nina   Yeah, coffee. Coffee's great. Thanks.

Roberto *goes off behind the counter.*

Nina   Is Roberto from Chile?

Maura   No, from El Salvador. He's a very good friend.

Nina   Maura. You never told me who's the father of your baby? Is it Roberto?

Maura   No, I think it is Wales man I met at Glastonbury Festival. I don't know. I try to find him. No problem. I want the baby.

Roberto *has reappeared with the coffees and a small case full of instruments. He sits down beside them and opens the case.*

Roberto   There we are. Okay.

He produces an instrument for testing blood pressure and attaches it to **Maura**'s *arm.*

Nina   What's this? What's going on?

Maura   Roberto is my doctor. I don't like hospitals.

Roberto (*by way of explanation*)   I am doctor, was a doctor in my country. (*Reading the blood pressure.*) But I keep telling her she must go to the hospital, too. You tell her, she never listens to me.

Nina   No. I have the same problem, Roberto.

Symonds (*OOV*)   Roberto!

Maura   Oh shit, the boss!

Symonds, *the owner, has emerged from the kitchen, looking thunderous.*

Symonds   Roberto!

Roberto   Just coming.

Symonds *comes over.*

Symonds   What's going on here?

Roberto   Nothing. I am just coming.

Symonds (*to* **Maura**)   I might have known you'd be involved.

Maura *shrugs.*

Symonds (*to* **Nina**)   Have you paid for these?

Nina   We haven't had the bill yet.

Symonds (*sour*)   Sure.

Nina   I'm sorry?

Symonds   Pull the other leg.

Nina   What?

Symonds   I've been looking at the till roll, looking at the bills, and counting the customers, and what do you know, they don't add up.

Maura   ¡De nuevo otra vez!

Symonds   I try to give you people a break. (*Hisses.*) It's a well known fact you're not meant to be working, but I don't ask any questions, and then, of course, I get diddled right under my nose.

Roberto   I'm sorry, you speak too quickly.

Symonds   I bet I do. Okay.

He looks round, a customer waits at the counter while a young waitress **Maura** *greeted when they came in, stands, transfixed by the confrontation.*

Symonds   I'll say it in words of one syllable. You people have been ripping me off, stealing my money, stitching me up, robbing me? Comprenez?

Roberto (*gravely*)   No!

Maura (*violent*)   !El no te está robando, pero lo debería hacer!

Roberto (*to* **Nina**)   No nos ha pagado el sueldo que nos había prometido cuando nos contrató. Nos dijo cuatro libras, pero nada más que nos ha pagado tres libras porque dice que no pagamos impuestos en este país.

Symonds   Can anybody speak the Queen's English here?

Nina I can. This man is saying you've been cheating him and all the other employees.

Symonds I bloody well have not.

Roberto Asi que tenemos un arreglo entre nosotros. Por cada hora que trabajamos cogemos una libra. Por ejemplo, no registramos el dinero de los cafés. Pero nunca cogemos más que esta libra que ves.

Symonds (*over this*) I bloody well have not been cheating them. I'm telling you, they're lucky I give them work, they're all here illegally. I can tell you that for nothing!

Nina (*to* **Symonds**) Can you shut up a minute! Okay. He's saying you promised them all four pounds an hour . . . which is pretty criminal, incidentally . . . and then you dock them a pound of that on some specious basis.

Symonds They're not paying tax! They come here and sponge off – 'cause I'm paying tax, I'm not exempt –

Nina (*interrupting*) I'd be very interested to know their legal position, anyway, what they're doing is paying themselves the extra pound, which is their money, by not ringing up the coffees, seems to make perfect sense to me.

Symonds (*over this*) Don't tell me about their legal position –

Roberto (*over this*) !Debíamos mandar a este cabrón a mi país. Le cortarían los cojones!

Symonds (*over this*) – 'Cause I could make one telephone call, and these lot would be down the police station! (*Turning on* **Roberto**.) I heard that, calling me a bastard! Don't think I don't understand a lot of what you're saying!

He shoves **Roberto**. **Roberto** *shoves him back. He shoves* **Roberto**, *who falls against the table. It's not funny.*

Nina (*flashing with anger*)   Come on. Watch it.

During this, **Mark,** *the young man with the meal and the novel, has been watching events with interest. He suddenly stands up.*

Mark (*a huge distraction*)   There is nothing up my left sleeve! There is nothing up my right sleeve! There is nothing on my plate except gravy. (*Traces the plate then licks his fingers.*) Yum. I take this novel, Russian, it must always be a Russian novel, and I throw it in the air.

He does so. As it flies from his hands it becomes a pigeon which flutters, anxious, then flaps out for freedom.

Roberto   !Increíble!

Mark (*a slight bow*)   Any chance of another coffee?

Ext: Street. Day.

Nina *and* **Maura** *approach.* **Mark**'s *car is parked. He gets out.*

Mark (*from the car*)   Would you like a lift?

Nina   We're fine, I think. Maura?

Maura   Sí, claro.

Nina   Thanks, anyway. And thanks, thanks for your performance, for intervening back there. It was pretty extraordinary.

Mark (*making light of it*)   Any excuse.

Nina   Is that your profession?

Mark   Magic? Oh no. No, no it's not. Uh . . .

He seems about to say something else.

Nina   What?

Mark   Nothing. Right, okay.

Nina   Bye.

He closes the passenger door and goes round to get into the driver's seat.

Nina *watches him, her interest tugged.*

Maura (*appreciatively, of* **Mark**)   Very fine person!

Ext: **Nina**'s *building. Early evening.*

As **Nina** *arrives home, laden up with stuff from work,* **George** *emerges from his van. Not quite what* **Nina** *had in mind.*

George   I'd been calling and calling.

Nina   George, hello.

George   Is that answer-machine working? Thought I'd better come round.

Nina   Oh dear, and have you been waiting?

George   I was getting a bit worried about you.

Nina   I'm fine.

George (*busy organising himself*)   Still bad in there, is it?

Nina   What?

George   In the flat . . .

Does a little scurrying mime along the front bonnet.

Nina   George, George, George, you're not going to believe this – they've gone.

George   Well, of course, they won't have gone, but good, good.

Nina   No, no, they've definitely gone. It's amazing.

George   Nina, ask me how many years I've been in Pest Control . . . and shall I tell you, like all wars, you develop a healthy respect for the enemy. Never underestimate him.

He's at the back of the van, getting out his suitcase and plastic gloves.

George   A rat is a highly intelligent creature, he's a formidable opponent.

Nina (*awkward*)   George, actually this is a really bad time, George. It's not a good time.

George   It's no problem. I don't need to stop. Five minutes in and out. That car's been here yonks. I've told you. It's gotta go. What's the matter?

Nina   Nothing, nothing, nothing. Come in, of course. I'll make you a cup of tea. I'll just – er . . .

She rings the bell to her own front door, long and hard.

Nina (*turning, shrugging to* **George**)   I always do that. Frighten off the ghosts.

And they go in.

Int: **Nina**'s *flat. Front door to kitchen corridor to bathroom corridor to kitchen. Evening.*

The front door opens, **Nina** *comes in,* **George** *shuffling behind her. She is not really listening to* **George** *as she scours the flat for* **Jamie***, whispering 'Jamie' under her breath.*

In passing she notes yet more alterations to the flat.

George   They lie low . . .

Nina   Jamie.

George   No, it's quite astonishing, they lie low, they won't touch the trays . . . So I clear off, and then they come back. They're not stupid.

Nina   No, no.

George   No, no you see your trays are untouched.
Your trays are untouched.

Nina   Mm.

George   You know, I think they talk to each other.

Nina   Jamie.

Nina's *gone from room to room. Nothing.*

George (*approaching*)   You've had a tidy up.

Nina   Yeah, (*shrugs.*) well, it needed it.

George   He's got a soft spot for you, you know.

Nina (*rather alarmed*)   Who?

George (*explaining*)   Titus. I've always been rather
fond of the Poles, myself.

Nina   Let me make the tea.

George   Lovely. Is it me or is it very hot in here?

Int: **Nina**'s *bedroom. Evening.*

George *knocks on and peers round the door.*

George   That's me. I'm off.

Nina   All right, George. Thanks for coming. And,
sorry if I was a bit unwelcoming.

George   You're a lovely girl.

Nina *smiles.*

George   I was telling my wife all about you.

Nina (*very surprised*)   Oh? Really? George, I'm sorry –
I thought your wife had died.

George (*nodding*)   1978. Still talk to her though. Tell
her my day. Don't you do that?

Nina   I do, yes.

George   'And death shall have no dominion.' We know that, you and me, eh?

*Int: **Nina**'s bathroom. Evening.*

Nina *is in the bath. She's finished her ablutions. She is wearing a face pack.*

She hums. It's a very private moment.

*A toy dolphin appears by **Nina**'s face. It eats the fish on a string.*

Nina   God!

Jamie's *face appears over the side of the bath.*

Jamie   Hi.

Nina *is absolutely shaken to find **Jamie** sitting at the edge of the tub.*

Nina   Don't do that! You scared me half to – ! Don't ever do that!

Jamie   Is this a bad time?

Nina *leaning back in the bath.*

Nina   It's a terrible time, Jamie. There are some things . . .

Jamie   Oh, come on, don't be coy.

Nina   I'm serious! Go away!

Jamie   Darling, I knew you shaved your legs.

Nina, *appalled at the epiphany that locked doors have no meaning any more.*

Nina   God, I can't even lock the door on you any more!

Jamie   I thought you might be pleased to see me.

Nina   No, I'm not.

Jamie *sulks. She scoops some bubbles out of the bath and puts them on his nose.*

Nina Yes, I am pleased, but just leave me alone for a bit. Of course I'm pleased to see you. I was terrified you'd gone.

They kiss.

Jamie See you later.

Nina Yep.

Jamie *goes to the door. It's locked.*

Jamie Why do you lock this?

Nina I don't know.

He's unlocked the door. As it opens, distant hubbub appears to be coming from another room.

Nina Have you turned the telly on?

Jamie (*uncomfortable*) Uh, yes. Um. Listen, sweetheart, don't get, but some of the guys wanted to come back and, just watch a couple of videos.

Nina What guys?

Jamie Friends, some friends . . .

Nina Dead friends?

Jamie (*casually*) I don't know, I suppose so, yes.

Nina Are you telling me there are dead people in my living room watching videos?

Jamie *shrugs.*

Nina (*irritated*) Well, I mean. Aren't there videos available wherever they are normally?

Jamie (*haughty*) Look if it's a problem, these are my friends, Nina, no, okay, I'll send them away, sure.

Nina No, it's fine. It's absolutely fine.

Jamie I'd forgotten you could be like this.

Nina   Be like what?

Jamie   Doesn't matter.

Nina   I said it's fine.

Jamie *sneezes.*

Nina   Bless you.

Jamie *sneezes.*

Nina   Bless you.

Jamie (*is this a cold coming!*)   Oh no.

He exits. A third sneeze. **Nina** *frowns, sinks back into the bath.*

Int: **Nina's** *flat – bathroom to hall to living room. Night.*

Four men are lounging male-like around the television, various ages, their antecedents hard to identify. They all wear warm coats. One of them, **Isaac,** *is talking about the film 'Easy Street' which they are watching.*

Nina *emerges from the bathroom, wrapped in a robe, and comes – apprehensively – into the living room.*

Jamie *gets up as* **Nina** *enters.*

Jamie   Oh, Nina. This is Freddie and this is Pierre. This is Bruno. And this is –

Isaac   Isaac.

Nina   Hello.

Jamie   Isaac. This is Nina.

Muted, polite hello's.

Nina (*awkward*)   Well, can I get anybody anything?

Muted, polite no's.

Bruno   The tape with 'Manhattan' written on it – it isn't.

Nina Oh no, you know, the other day I was trying to record 'Hannah and Her Sisters' . . .

Bruno It's a lovely film.

Nina . . . on the end and I think, I've got a terrible feeling – (*Turns to* **Jamie**.) I'm so hopeless with that machine.

Jamie You haven't recorded over it! Nina. . . ! (*To the others*.) She did that with 'Strangers on a Train'!

Bruno Really? What a drag!

Isaac I love 'Strangers on a Train'.

So do the others.

Freddie He's wonderful in that, isn't he?

Isaac Fantastic.

Nina Sorry.

Bruno That's such a drag.

Nina Sorry.

Jamie *puts a finger to her temple like a pistol and pulls the trigger.*

Int: **Nina's** *living room. Night.*

Later. And 'Brief Encounter' is finishing on the television. The ghosts are moved. They share blankets and Kleenex in the darkened room.

Nina's *asleep on the settee.* **Jamie** *next to her.*

Isaac *jumps up.*

Isaac Okay, 'Five Easy Pieces' or 'Fitzcarraldo'?

Various voices. **Nina** *wakes up.*

Nina Guys, guys. Actually, I'm going to have to go to bed.

A muted chorus of goodnights. **Jamie** *kisses* **Nina.**

Jamie   I'll be in in a minute.

Nina (*to* **Jamie**)   Don't be long.

Isaac (*on the next film*)   Let's take a vote.

Int: **Nina'***s bedroom. Night.*

Jamie *stumbles into the bedroom and clambers into the bed. He rescues the pile of quilts which have fallen onto the floor.*

Jamie (*sliding against* **Nina**)   Mmm, you smell so nice.

Nina (*asleep but agreeable*)   Nnngggh.

Jamie   Were you asleep?

Nina   Nnngggh.

They snuggle up.

Jamie   Nina, have we still got that hot water bottle?

Nina   Oh, Jamie, the thing is I'm so hot, I'm suffocating, I'm too hot.

Jamie   Okay, don't worry, don't worry, I love you, sshhh, go back to sleep.

He sneezes.

Jamie   The guys are nice, aren't they?

Nina   Nnnghhh.

He sneezes.

Jamie   Great guys.

Ext: Bus stop on London street. Day.

Nina *waiting for a bus to go to* **Burge'***s – her therapist's – house.*

*The bus draws up. A group of mentally handicapped
teenagers and young adults start to get off the bus.
Showing the way is* **Mark**. **Anthony**, *one of the group, is
getting off as* **Nina** *gets on to the bus.*

Nina *sees* **Mark** *and greets him. She's pleased to see him
again.*

Nina Oh, hi.

Mark, *delighted to see her.*

Mark Hello!

Nina How are you?

Mark Fine, fine. This is Anthony. Anthony, this is
my friend uh –

Nina Nina.

Mark Nina.

Anthony Hello Nina.

Nina Hello.

Mark We're going for a walk, we're going to do some
painting and have a picnic.

Anthony Do you want to come?

Nina Uh . . .

Mark I think Nina's probably busy.

Nina No, actually I'd like to, I'd love to, but I; I've
got an appointment. I'm late.

Mark Well, nice to see you.

Anthony *knows the catchphrase.*

Anthony To see you nice!

Nina Yeah. You too.

Mark How's your friend, by the way, who's having
the baby?

Nina Oh, Maura? She's fine, fine . . .

Mark, *suddenly aware that his group is dispersing.*

Mark   No, don't disappear. Helen! Adrian! Just – (*He turns to* **Nina**.) I'd better go.

Nina   Okay. Okay. Bye.

Mark *and his group head off up a path.* **Nina** *goes to sit on the bus.*

Mark (*OOV*)   Nina! Nina!

Nina *stands up.* **Mark** *has come back to the side of the bus.*

Mark   Sorry.

Nina *winds down the window.*

Mark   Look, uh, I was wondering, do you think maybe sometime we could, this is probably terrible, you say no but –

Nina   Yes, I'd like to.

Mark (*delighted, surprised*)   Oh, really!

Nina   Yes.

Mark   Well, can I call you?

Nina   Uh, yes. No. No, no, I'll call you.

Mark (*disappointed*)   Okay.

Nina   No, I will call, it's just, have you got a pen?

Mark   Yeah. I think so. No. Don't go away.

He sprints back to his group. By this time **Mark**'s *whole party have assembled to watch the proceedings. They smile at* **Nina**.

Mark *gets a pen and hares back to* **Nina**.

Mark   I haven't got any paper.

Nina *holds her hand out of the bus window.*

Nina   Doesn't matter. Write on that.

Mark   261 0840. Or you can get me at work. 267 – I can't remember.

Nina   That's fine.

Mark   'Bye.

Nina   'Bye.

He goes back to the good-natured observations of his charges. **Mark** *waves. The whole group waves.*

Int: **Burge's** *office. Day.*

Nina *on the settee.*

Nina   I was reading, uh. I was reading and must have been one of those books you lent me on, about bereavement, and it was about how it's possible some people might get this sen – this powerful sensation that their loved one has come back, I don't mean like a *sense* of their presence – an abstract thing. I mean, you know, they they've *actually come back* and are in their house. Well, what do you think about that? Is that ridiculous?

There is a long pause.

Burge   What? Is what ridiculous?

Nina   I don't know, that . . . well, when I read this, I thought – how ridiculous! I mean –

Burge   Why?

Music: Bach: Brandenburg No 3, 1st Movement.

Nina   Well, no, I can imagine it. I mean, I can imagine going home this evening and there's Jamie. And he's back –

Burge (*prompting*)   All right.

Nina   – but then, but then what?

Int: **Nina's** *living room. Night.*

Nina *kneels at the open window. The music swells.*

Burge (*VO*) What you are saying is ridiculous?

Nina, *dizzy with her predicament.*

Nina (*VO*) Well – oh, I don't know, I don't know, everything, everything, everything. I don't know. I don't know.

Nina *closes the window and sits down to reveal* **Jamie,** *and a dozen other musicians, giving a performance of the Bach Brandenburg.*

Nina *is concentrating, moved, but tight, feeling claustrophobic.*

There are a dozen other members of the audience scattered around the room, on the floor, squashed on the settee, including **Isaac, Bruno** *and* **Freddie.**

Apart from the overcoats and scarves it could be a neo-Victorian Chamber Evening.

Jamie *catches* **Nina's** *eye. Smiles. She smiles back, tries to look calm, but she's in turmoil.*

The music soars.

Ext: The south bank. Early evening.

The river. **Mark** *is waiting patiently for* **Nina** *– who, late, hurrying, finally turns up.*

Nina (*as she approaches*) I'm sorry, I'm sorry, I'm sorry. Oh God. I'm so sorry.

Mark, *ever the magician, pulls a bunch of blood red roses from his jacket.*

Mark (*with a flourish*) Madam.

Then flinching, as if from the thorns, and feeling inside his shirt.

Mark Ouch. Sorry –

Nina Oh, they're glorious, thank you, they're, the scent!

Then, of their date – they were off to the National Theatre.

Nina I'm sorry, I know it's ridiculously, it's started hasn't it, but I –

Mark (*calming*) It doesn't matter. We can do something else.

Nina No, I can't. I can't.

Mark Why? Has something happened?

Nina I have to be somewhere else. It's very complicated.

Mark (*now openly deflated*) Okay.

Nina No, listen. It's complicated but not for, I guarantee whatever you're thinking is not why it's complicated. Truly.

Mark What am I going to tell my group? They're on tenterhooks.

Nina Is that, is – are they your work?

Mark (*by way of saying yes*) We were drawing trees, you know, you draw a tree and then you draw in the roots and the branches and you put in all the names which are important, have you got time for this?

Nina Of course, sure, I just haven't –

Mark, *he's drawing an imaginary tree.*

Mark Okay, you draw a tree and then on the roots of the tree you put the people who were important in forming you, or stabilising you, or taking care of you . . . Mum, Dad, sister . . . whoever, and then you put in the names of people who are around you now and – this is on the branches, like leaves. Sorry, are you with me?

Nina Yes, I think so.

Mark And I did, I was painting my own tree, and Anthony, who you met, Anthony was looking at my tree and he suddenly said, *well where's Nina?* Actually, it's not just my group who's on tenterhooks, but, anyway can I give you a lift?

Nina No, really. I'll be fine.

Mark Aren't we both going north? I could just drop you at the end of the road. It would be –

Nina I'll get a bus. Really. It's better if I – You can walk me to the Underground . . . if you want . . .

They walk in silence. Then after a while.

Mark (*attempting to see the funny side*) This is my shortest ever date. Yours?

Nina Yes.

Mark That's something, then. (*Dry.*) Are you interested in my last name? Or – no, no, hang on – stop!

Nina What?

He stops her and maps out a course.

Mark Okay. Okay. Look, this is what we do. I tell you everything about my life between here and that statue there. See it? . . . we hop of course . . . and then you tell me everything about yours. No lies from the speaker, no interruptions, no questions from the listener. And I'm off:

He hops, he begins at full tilt.

Mark Mark Damian de Grunwald, born Budleigh Salterton, 32 next birthday, Capricorn, don't believe in that – that's star signs I mean, parents alive, retired, father silent practically completely silent, eighteen years older than my mother who is not, completely silent, owned a mill, then a post office, then a tea shop, amateur magician, father that is, and I was his assistant

at Conservative Club Dinner Dances, regularly sawn in
half from the age of seven, and made to disappear in
ideologically unsound circumstances. Change legs. What
else? Home: okay, puberty: okay, parents: okay, one
brother: okay, academically: okay, vaguely asthmatic
attempted suicide at seventeen, can't remember why, I
was sad about something, aspirins, stomach pump,
followed by weekly sessions with educational
psychologist for whom I developed an enormous
passion and encouraged me to become a psychologist
myself, A levels, Psychology degree at Sussex
University, trained in Art Therapy, what is Art
Therapy? You draw trees. Have one daughter, Gemma,
seven, that should come earlier, uh, lived with Gemma's
mother for three weeks before she left me for theology
student, I've stopped believing in God, but long enough
with me to get pregnant. Gemma is seven, did I say
that already? And her hair is curly and has red sparks,
you know, in the sun, and she calls me Mark de
Grunwald and the vicar she calls Daddy and –

The statue looms.

Mark I love, basically everything – you know: music,
curry, I can practically recite the collected works of

A few hops from the statue.

Mark Oh hello. And I live alone and my fridge is
empty and I wash my own clothes and I'm interested in
Nina who is not on my tree and I can do magic. And
now you go. And straight away. Yes. Don't think. Go!

Nina *looks at him. She likes, is confused, intrigued by this
biographical sketch. She hesitates.*

Nina (*wavering*) I can't.

Mark Yes.

Nina Er –

And she plunges in.

Nina   Nina Mitchell –

Mark (*interrupting*)   You've got to hop, you've got to
hop!

She hops.

Nina   Nina Mitchell, I can't believe I'm doing this!
Also Capricorn, but also don't believe so I can't make
anything of that, think there may be a God, interpreter,
I'm starting at the end, I believe in protesting, in the
possibility of change, in making this planet more,
decent. You know, you see it all the time. I hate what
this country is doing to itself, and to the people, and the
way we treat other races, visitors, this happens every
day . . . well you know, you saw it in the cafe . . .
wrong skin, wrong size, wrong shape: you're lost . . . or
wrong religion, wrong ideology, wrong class, it makes
me so! Oh, do you want me to be more personal? Um,
okay, parents alive, Gloucestershire, teachers, him
Geography, her History, so holidays it would be *Dad,*
where are we? Mum, have we been here before? I like
them, I have a sister, Claire, I love her, she has a family
and a husband I can't stand who keeps climbing
everything – climbs socially, in business, and now –
finally – has started climbing mountains. Um, they have
a son, Harry. She's pregnant again for the second time,
their son is my nephew, and I adore him. Did I say I
was born in Stratford? Well, I was and do you know
that I pay to do this once a week, to talk, that's where I
was going the other day when I saw you on the bus, to
my woman, the Burge, Doctor Burge. The only
difference is there you get fifty minutes and no exercise
and here it seems to spill out, and I play the piano, I
love Bach, I have rats, I'm in a mess, I live alone, I
haven't always, not always –

There is a busker playing. The music pulls her as she talks,
he's playing one of the Bach Sarabands.

Something causes **Nina** *to turn and look. It's* **Jamie**! *She stops, dumbfounded.*

Mark Hey! Come on Nina. You're not hopping. Come on.

Nina, *oblivious, has turned and walked towards the busker. It's not* **Jamie**.

Nina *watches for a few seconds.*

Ext: **Nina's** *street and house. Night.*

As **Nina** *approaches, she can hear* **Jamie** *practising his cello in the living room. She loves him, feels badly. She has the roses with her. She dumps them into a rubbish bin.*

Int: **Nina's** *living room. Night.*

Nina *comes in.* **Jamie** *stops playing. It is the Bach Saraband.*

Nina (*genuine*) I love you. Don't stop.

Jamie (*gently*) Where've you been?

Nina Nowhere, nowhere, work.

Jamie You're so late.

Nina I know. Sorry.

Jamie I got worried.

Nina Sorry.

Jamie (*wry*) Just like old times.

Nina *and* **Jamie** *consider each other. The room seems large without the crew of spirits.*

Jamie Is there something you want to tell me?

Nina I have this feeling you're with me, are you with me all day?

Jamie No.

Nina I think of you as being on my shoulder, and if you're there, then you'll know I am like someone who carries their loved one on their shoulder . . . if that was what you were asking . . .

Jamie I'm not, but thank you.

Nina Excuse me, where is my television? And the video machine!

Jamie Oh, right, I put them in our bedroom because people couldn't get comfortable in here, it's so cold in the evenings, and, and anyway I wanted to play and – don't worry they'll move when we want to go to bed, it's no problem, don't get frazzled.

Nina (*frustrated*) Oh please.

Jamie Nina, you can't come home in the middle of the night and then complain I've got company.

Nina It's not the middle of the night! I don't know these people. I don't know, I don't even know what period they're from. This is ridiculous!

Jamie You could try talking to them.

Nina I can't believe this is happening! I've got ghosts watching videos in my bedroom and I'm being accused – of what? What am I being accused of? Jamie, they're dead people! The rats have gone, now I'm infested with ghosts!

Jamie There are eight or nine people in there, they're not doing you any harm. If you want to go to bed, they'll go. Just tell them. If you want me to go, just tell me.

Nina And why are they all men! I don't want you to go, darling. I don't want you to go! I don't know what I want. Anyway, I bought you a hot water bottle. Do you want it?

She pulls a hot water bottle out of her bag. It's shaped like a pig. **Jamie** *inspects it. He's pleased.*

Jamie Thanks. It's great.

He comes behind her and puts his arms round her.

Nina I mean, why can't you go back to, to Heaven! while I'm at work?

Jamie I don't know. It's like you make a choice and then you, I don't know. I'm here. It's fine. It's fine. I love you.

He scrapes his cheek against her.

Jamie Smooth?

They laugh. **Freddie**'s *head comes round the door.*

Freddie Hello, Nina, I thought I heard you, did you remember to go to the – ?

The sound of 'The Lavender Hill Mob' comes from the bedroom.

Nina *rummaging, pulling out videos.*

Nina They didn't have 'I Vitelloni' but I got 'Pinocchio' and 'Forget Venice'.

Freddie Fantastic! Have you seen that, Jamie? 'Forget Venice'? Fantastic. So tender. By the way Isaac says you're in check. It's your move. It looks bad.

Jamie (*getting up*) I can't be! How can I be in check? Hang on a second sweetheart.

And **Jamie**'s *off.* **Nina** *sits on the arm of the settee. She leans across and plucks the strings of the cello.*

Int: **Nina**'s *hall. Night.*

It's the middle of the night and the telephone is ringing.

Nina *stumbles into the corridor.*

Freddie, *sleeping nearest to the telephone, picks up the receiver, doesn't answer it, but holds it out, frowning with sleep, to* **Nina,** *who trips over a sleeping body or two on her way to the receiver.*

Nina *winces, a kicked body groans and turns over.*

Nina   Oh. Sorry. Thanks, Freddie. (*Into receiver.*) Oh God. Hello, yeah. Yeah. Okay. Of course. Yeah, I'll come.

She's learning that **Maura** *has gone prematurely into labour and that she's given the hospital admin.* **Nina's** *name as next of kin.*

Int: Maternity side room. Night.

Maura *is in a side room prior to going into a delivery room. The* **Midwife** *is with her.*

Nina *hurries in to her.*

Nina   Maura, querida.

Maura   Hola. Gracias por venir. Perdona la hora, pero la guagua está a punto de llegar.

Nina   No, está bien, está bien. ¿Cómo estás? Yo estoy contentísima, emocionada. ¿Y tú?

Maura   Estoy muerta de miedo.

Nina   Yo tambien. Me han dicho que todo esta bien.

Maura *gets a contraction. She squeezes* **Nina's** *hand.*

Nina   Hello, I'm Maura's friend. How is she?

Midwife   She's fine. She'll be going in to the delivery room any minute.

Maura   ¡Ven conmigo!

Nina   She wants me to come with her, can I?

Midwife   I don't see why not.

Nina Is everything, everything is, is it all – ?

Midwife Don't worry.

Nina Oh! Listen. Excuse me. Have you talked to her about medication, because, I mean have you given her any drugs or what?

Midwife She hasn't had anything yet. She can have gas and air, or pethidine, or whatever she wants.

Nina Hang on, can I just check with her, because I don't think that. (*Switching in mid-breath.*) Oye Maura, ¿quieres un calmante? Te van a ofrecer unas drogas para el dolor, ¿las quieres?

Maura Yes. Drugs. Give me drugs!

Nina (*a little deflated*) Well she thinks she does, at the moment, you know, but –

Maura *is crying.*

Nina Hey, what's the matter? ¿Qué te pasa?

Maura Titus. Yo quiero que Titus esté aquí también.

Nina ¿Quién? Perdona Maura, ¿quién?

Maura Titus. Yo quiero que Titus esté aquí.

Nina (*taken aback*) ¿Titus? ¿De verdad? Bueno . . .

Midwife Titus, yes, she's said that name several times. Is that the father?

Maura Titus me ama. Te lo quería contar, pero no te he visto.

Nina He loves you? Oh, does he? That's nice.

Midwife Okay, we can go in now.

Maura Titus. Quiero que venga. Quiero que venga. Titus. Titus. Titus.

Maura *is wheeled off, calling for* **Titus**.

Int: Delivery room. Early dawn.

Titus *and* **Nina** *encourage* **Maura** *over the final hurdles.
It's all happening. Triumph on three faces.*

Int: Side ward. Early dawn.

Titus *is asleep beside* **Maura**.

Maura *has been feeding her baby. She hands her over to*
Nina.

Nina   Qué linda, qué linda, qué linda. (*Tearful.*) A
new life, a new life. Hello. Hello, darling.

She kisses the **Baby**'s *forehead.*

Nina   A new life.

Int: **Nina**'s *hall. Day.*

As **Nina** *lets herself into the flat,* **Freddie** *and another
ghost are dragging a bookcase into an already crowded
hallway.*

Nina   What's going on?

Freddie   Hi Nina . . . (*To the other ghost, managing the
manoeuvre.*) Just hang on a minute.

They set the bookcase down with a grunt. **Freddie** *dusts
down his hands.*

Freddie   So tell me, was it a boy or a girl?

Nina   Girl.

Freddie (*excited*)   A girl! It was a girl! (*Calling.*)
Pierre? Pierre!

Pierre *appears.*

Freddie   Maura had a little girl.

Pierre (*thrilled*)   Tremendous.

Freddie (*to* **Nina**)   Was it moving? Isn't birth
moving?

Nina   Freddie, what's going on with the furniture?

Freddie   Oh, it's going to be great. Jamie took a look
at the floorboards in there and they're fabulous, they're
beautiful, they're those Victorian boards, we're just
getting the carpet – even as we speak!

Nina *goes past* **Freddie** *and negotiates the obstacle course
to the door to the living room.*

Int: **Nina**'s *living room. Day.*

Nina *enters just in time to see the carpet roll by her feet,
pushed by* **Jamie** *and company.*

Jamie   Hi! (*To his crew.*) Good work.

Kneeling to inspect the revealed floorboards.

Jamie   We just need to scrub this up a bit. It's oak. Is
it oak?

Isaac   It's definitely a hard wood.

Jamie   – or ash?

Nina (*absolutely exasperated*)   Jamie, what are you
doing?

Jamie   Aren't these boards amazing? Who would have
thought under that disgusting carpet . . . you need to
burn it by the way . . . it's full of mildew and silverfish,
but these boards! So, it was a girl.

Nina   I liked that carpet.

Jamie   Don't be perverse.

Nina   Well, I did like it and you can't just go around
pulling, treating my flat as –

Jamie   Nina, the carpet was threadbare, it is
threadbare, and it's full of mould and mildew and . . .

and these boards, even you must acknowledge that,
these are in a different – !

Nina (*raging*) I feel like I'm being burgled! Every
time I come home I feel like I've been burgled!

Jamie What?

He frowns at the others.

Nina (*flailing*) Oh God. The flat – chairs are moved!
The the the . . . pictures are different, they're not
where, and, it's my flat! It's my flat! I mean – !

Jamie Do you want to have a row in public? It's
actually quite embarrassing for everybody . . . for me
. . . and uh . . .

He turns and shrugs to his mates.

Nina Well no, I don't, no I don't want to be in public
in my own home. That's right. That's absolutely right!
So, in fact, could your friends go, please, could
everybody just go, do you think? Is that possible? That
I could have some time in my, now! Now! Please. Is
that, is that asking too much?

Jamie (*to his cronies*) Sorry.

*The **Ghosts** leave, rather sulkily. **Nina** and **Jamie** alone.*

Jamie (*furious*) Satisfied?

Then he sneezes, dramatically, repeatedly.

Nina (*acidly*) It's only dust.

Jamie Nina, that was really humiliating. You ask
people to give you a hand, they don't need to, they lug
your furniture around half the day and then you come
back and throw a tantrum. That was really really really
humiliating.

He sneezes again. It settles in silence.

Nina (*desperate, floundering*) Was it like this before?

Jamie (*as he blows his nose*) What?

Nina Before, were we like this?

Jamie What? Like what? Look, you're tired, your
friend just had a baby, you were up half the night, it's
traumatic, it's an emotional experience, let's not turn
that into –

Nina Tell me about the first night we spent together.

Jamie Why? Seriously? You want me to?

Nina What did we do?

Jamie We talked.

Nina What else?

Jamie Well, talking was the major component! Uh,
uh, we, you played the piano – and I played and we
both played a duet – something, I can't remember . . .
and you danced for about three hours until I fell asleep,
but you were fantastic! – and then we had some
cornflakes and when we kissed – which was about
eleven o'clock the following day – we were trembling so
much we couldn't take off our clothes.

*They remember. They're both sitting now on the bare
boards. Quiet. Closer.*

Nina You see, I held that baby – so

She makes a tangible gesture.

It's life, it's a life I want. And, and, and all my taste
. . . my things, after you died. I found stuff in my trunk
I'd put there because you disapproved or laughed at
them – books and photographs and I couldn't, I didn't
know how to mend a fuse or find a plumber or bleed a
radiator but – and now I do. It is a ridiculous flat, but
I'll get there, it'll be beautiful, it could be, I think it
could be. I, I, I – I so much longed for you, I longed
for you.

Jamie How's your Spanish?

Nina What?

Jamie There's a poem I wanted you to translate. I read it, there's a bit that I wanted to tell you, I wanted you to hear –

Nina Okay.

Jamie *recites an extract from the poem, 'The Dead Woman' by Pablo Neruda.*

Jamie Uh – Perdóname.

Nina (*translating*) Forgive me . . .

Jamie Si tú no vives,

Nina I know this poem. If you are not living . . .

Jamie Si tú, querida, amor mío,
Si tu te has muerto

Nina If you, beloved, my love,
If you have died

Jamie Todas las hojas caerán en mi pecho

Nina All the leaves will fall on my breast

Jamie Lloverá sobre mi alma noche y día

Nina It will rain on my soul, all night, all day

Jamie Mis piés querrán marchar hacia donde tú duermes

Nina My feet will want to march to where you are sleeping. Your accent's terrible.

Jamie Pero seguiré vivo

Nina *gets up and goes to* **Jamie**.

Nina My feet will want to march to where you are sleeping but I shall go on living.

Jamie Do you want me to go?

She clings to him.

Nina No, never, never, never, never, never.

*Ext: Outside **Nina**'s flat. Day.*

Nina *comes out of the flat.*

Int: **Nina**'s *living room. Day.*

Jamie *is still sitting on the floor of the living room. The others pile in.*

Freddie (*apprehensive*)   Well?

Jamie *shrugs, gives them a sad smile.*

Jamie   I think so, yes.

Freddie's *kind compassionate smile.*

Ext: Bridge. Day.

Nina *walks across the bridge.*

Ext: Cafe. Day.

Nina *sits at a table outside the cafe with a cup of coffee.*

Ext: Mental Handicap Centre. Day.

Nina *makes her way into the building where* **Mark** *works.*

Inside she sees **Mark** *with his group. There's some sort of activity going on.* **Nina** *finds their movements simple, uncluttered – intolerably moving.*

Mark *spots her, comes to the window. He's a little wary. He looks at her. She shrugs. She beams and mimes incomprehensibly. He beams and mimes incomprehensibly.*

Then **Anthony** *and the others come to the window. They wave.* **Nina** *waves back.*

Ext: Mental Handicap Centre car park. Day.

Mark *and* **Nina** *make their way towards his car.*

Mark   We could see a film.

Nina   Okay.

Mark (*wry*)   Or we could try the play again?

Nina   Okay.

Mark   Or we could, we could just go home and eat.

Nina (*benign*)   Anything.

They've reached the car. He opens her door and goes round to open his door. **Nina** *leans against the door and starts to cry.* **Mark** *goes round to her.*

Nina   I'm sorry, I'm going to cry, and it's not going to make any sense and I feel really . . . I'm so sorry.

Mark   I've sort of worked out you're living with somebody, I mean I'm not a private detective but you won't tell me where you live, you won't give me your number, so –

Nina   No, I'm not, I'm really not living with anybody.

Mark   You know, because if you're, if you're not free I think – because to be quite honest I'm in trouble here.

He means he's hooked.

Mark   I'm, I could embarrass myself.

Nina   I think I am free. I did love someone very much, you see. Very much. But he died. He died. And I've found it quite hard to get over it.

Mark   Well, why don't we just go home? If you want you could talk, you can tell me whatever, anything, everything.

Nina   Okay. Yeah.

They get into the car.

Ext.:/Int: **Mark**'s *car. Night.*

Mark's *car goes across the bridge.*

They're driving. They're squeezed up together, very close, smiling.

Nina (*suddenly*) Oh, could you stop, could you stop? Please. Stop.

Mark Sh, sure.

Mark *stops the car. He looks really deflated.*

Mark Are you all right?

Nina *dashes from the car, leaves her door swinging. We don't go with her, but stay on* **Mark**'s *disappointment. He thumps the steering wheel in frustration and then she's suddenly jumping back into the car.*

Nina Okay.

Mark What was all that about?

He looks perplexed. She holds up a toothbrush in its packet.

Nina (*shy*) It's not a threat.

She snuggles up.

Int: **Mark**'s *flat – living room to bathroom to bedroom. Night.*

Music: Bach's Keyboard Concerto No 7, Andante.

The dead of night.

The dining table has the remains of spaghetti, some wine. The bathroom has a new toothbrush.

Mark *and* **Nina** *are in bed.*

*Int: **Nina**'s flat – hall to bedroom to living room to
bathroom. Dawn.*

Nina *lets herself in.*

Music: Bach Sonata No 3 for cello and piano.

She hurries from room to room. **Jamie**'s *not there.*

*The living room is completely empty save for the piano
and the cello and a vase with **Mark**'s blood red roses
somehow salvaged.*

Nina   Jamie. Jamie. Jamie.

*Int:/Ext: **Nina**'s living room. Morning.*

Nina, *changed, showered, sits in the empty living room.
She watches the clouds sail by. She closes the window.*

*Int: **Nina**'s living room. Morning.*

Nina *kneels on the floor and scrubs the floorboards. A
soapy bucket beside her.*

A rat appears on the mantelpiece. They regard each other.

*Int: **Nina**'s hall and living room. Early evening.*

Nina *reverently puts **Jamie**'s cello into its case.*

She dials a telephone number. **Mark**'s.

Nina   Hi. It's me. Can you come and get me?

Mark (*VO*)   Oh hi. Er, no, I can't. Sorry.

Nina   Oh, okay.

Mark (*VO*)   Because actually I don't know where you
live. Bit of a problem.

Nina   It's 6A Ellingham Road.

Mark (*VO*)   Where's that?

Nina   N6.

Mark (*VO*)   Highgate. Okay. What, shall I come now, or what?

Nina   Okay.

Mark (*VO*)   Right. I'm on my way. Pack your toothbrush.

The music takes over. The Andante from Bach's keyboard Concerto No 7, a celebration.

Ext: Outside **Nina**'s *flat. Night.*

Mark's *car drives up.*

The music continues.

Int: **Nina**'s *living room. Night.*

Nina *looks around the room, the boards, the cello, the roses. Turns out the light. Goes out.*

The music continues.

Jamie *and the* **Ghosts** *file across the room towards the window.*

Ext: Outside **Nina**'s *flat. Night.*

Nina *emerges in a jacket.* **Mark** *has come out. She goes to him. They embrace.*

At the window of the front room the **Ghosts** *have assembled. They fill the window.* **Jamie,** *surrounded by* **Freddie, Pierre, Isaac, Bruno** *and co, watches as* **Nina** *embraces her lover. He is smiling and crying all at once. So are his friends who clap his back and support him, hand slaps of salute. It's a victory.*

Jamie's *face is awash with tears.*

The music plays.

Mosaic

Mosaic was performed as part of BBC2's *Dancelines* series in 1992 as a dance text for two women. One speaks but doesn't dance; one dances but doesn't speak.

Performers	Juliet Stevenson
	Lauren Potter
Choreographer	Jonathan Lunn
Director	Peter Munford

A WOMAN SPEAKS:

he stopped at the crossing
the woman was crying
I for some reason I for some reason

when I should have been somewhere else
a cafe
when you should have been somewhere else

for some reason
the phone goes dead
hello?

the branches swayed
in and out of my view
like arms

I'm sorry, I'm delayed, I can't get home.
You left the house
and you were singing

He didn't see me
he was driving
he stopped at the crossing
and I walked past him
he didn't see me
there was someone in the car with him
I didn't recognise.
A woman

the woman was crying

I for some reason I for some reason I
and I didn't tell my mother

I still don't know
who the woman was
why she was in my father's car
or why she was crying

years later
when I should have been somewhere else
I saw you in a cafe
when you should have been somewhere else
and for some reason for some reason

you were smoking a cigarette
and the chair opposite you was pushed at an angle
as if

you didn't see me
I waited
and you left

The phone rings sometimes
and I pick it up
and
for some reason
no-one answers
I say hello,
and there's a pause
and the line goes dead

Once I lived on a hill
and with binoculars
with my father's binoculars
from my room
I could see into the kitchen of a flat opposite me
and one evening
for an hour
for at least an hour
I watched a couple

while they cooked a meal
ate it
and washed up
the man wore yellow rubber gloves
and the bowl was the most brilliant of blues

it was a windy night
and branches swayed in and out of my view
like arms
the first time it happened
I was sure it was you
your arms
how could I have explained?
when I can't explain

Do you remember the game I played?
when I called you and said
I'm sorry, I'm delayed, I can't get home
and I was a hundred yards away at the call box
I won't be home until tomorrow
and I ran to surprise you and
then
and then
I for some reason I
for some reason
and then ten minutes later
you left the house
and you were singing!

the man plunging his hands into the bowl
the woman weeping in the car
the phone goes dead,
hello? hello?
you are singing as you skip from our door
the way the chair in the cafe was turned
the branches like arms

for some reason
I for some reason I
know someone had been sitting
ten years old, the satchel scuffing my raincoat
a woman crying in our car

my father's face, turned
the song, something, can't remember
the blue bowl
the chair, tilted, warm, I know it would be warm to the
    touch
the dead log of the phone

imagine filling your fist with dust
and flinging it into the room

I for some reason I
for some reason
have never
seen a pattern in these things.

Days Like These

Days Like These was performed as a short film for Comic Relief in 1989.

Performer	Liz Smith
Director	Paul Weiland

*An old woman is speaking to us, her face full in the frame,
her voice natural and thoughtful, rather unemphatic. A
conversation as if the listener were near and familiar and
benign.*

The **Woman** *sounds as if she were searching for something
in her experience, some kind of explanation for the
situation she finds herself in.*

Woman   Once, just to see, really, just as a kind of
experiment, I tried to see how long I could go without
speaking, I mean without having to speak, without
being called upon to say anything.
Nine days.
That was for the Postman.
He had a parcel for the little girl next door,
it was from Canada, and they were all out.
He said, 'You wouldn't mind signing for this, would
you?'
and I said, 'No'
'No', I said, after nine days. 'No'.

When I think how we used to read poetry to each other,
all those words we must have said out loud,
hundreds of words,
long poems, before we went to sleep,
he used to like a military poem, or an adventure
I preferred a lilt, a nice lilt . . .
you want ones which rhyme, of course, because they
give you a steady jog to go at
di dum di dum di dum di dum
he had a marvellous laugh, my husband, if you just
heard his voice you could have measured him by that
laugh,
a big broad-beamed laugh,
I try not to think of it
I try not to remember it
I try not to remember a lot of things
but especially the laugh

he died laughing
it's funny the thing which should make me weep
after all this time
is the memory of his laugh

He was sitting in front of the fire
we'd just got the fire, the gas fire, and we were
experimenting sitting in front of it
we'd had so many years of a proper fire
so we were sat there and he made a joke about the
setting
you could set it at Miser Rate,
– it had that written on it: *Miser Rate* –
which meant not fully on,
so we set it at Miser Rate
and he made this joke, I can't remember it
and he started to laugh
and in the middle of the laugh
he died
he said
actually I feel quite cold
and then fell forward
anyway
I never liked that fire because I thought it was an insult
to people who couldn't afford to keep the fire on full
to call it Miser Rate
no-one who'd been cold
not cold after a swim or a walk or
just cold, cold all day
would call it Miser Rate
from things like that
you know that modern life is now the province of the
young
the busy young
no time to live, no time to die

The first day you don't have to have the fire on
each year that's a lovely day I think
the clocks go forward

you can sit in a park at five o'clock and it's all right
and you know for ages it's only going to get better,
more and more light until those gorgeous summer
evenings with just a cardigan and the window open –
no, but for me the first few days of Spring are best,
the smell of mown lawns
you can dry a blouse out on the line
and the children start playing outside
which is a lovely noise
children playing outside
not at all the same as the sound of children playing
indoors
which is a muffled sound as if they were cooped up
which they are really
I don't think you ever hear the proper sound of a child
indoors

I've always liked the young
their bright voices and their bright clothes
and their loudness
everything about them is so loud
which I think is rather wonderful, actually,
their love affairs and their parties and their motorcars
and their children and their music
except
nothing makes you feel more alone than other people's
noise
and the louder it is the more lonely you feel
the LIFE which goes on next door
the tramping up and down the hall
the bicycles
the slamming of the blasted front door
the rows
the tears
the sheer LIFE
God!

nothing replaces the sound of another voice
or touch

I mean even being shouted at or argued with
or
– wonderful really –
someone else's mess
having to make two cups of tea
or
it's funny, he used to have terribly cheesy feet, terrible!
I used to go on about that, I used to put them outside.
for years after he'd gone I kept a pair of his shoes, his
brown work ones, and I could smell them
the things you do!
then one day it had gone, nothing
you would have thought I'd gone a bit bats
kneeling at this cupboard smelling an old brown
shoe . . .

I don't want people to pity me
because I've had a life
I've been kissed and courted
and jilted
and I've danced and danced
and stayed out too late
and lied to my lovers
and memorised songs and
had my children
and laid out a husband
I don't want to be pitied
put the laughs I've had end to end there would be
months of laughter
a lot of it wicked
but I would love never to do another jigsaw
I would love to be visited
to be put to some use
I would love to be part of that big fat loud life going on
outside the window
because I think this is not the way to deal
with people
this can't be the way
if you went in my street now, the whole city,

and you had a great big tin opener
and you could just cut off the roofs like opening up a
tin of salmon or
and then looked down at us from up above
the people would look like
what would we look like?
one person in each room
trying not to remember the thing which brings tears to
their eyes
while the busy young
try not to remember they'll be old
that it's the most natural thing in the world
that like a poet we used to love said about life
he said if you thought of each ten years as a day
life lasted about a week
look at life like that and
at thirty you're already on Wednesday,

so I regret there is no use for me that people see
that I must pounce on the milkman like a cat for a lick
of conversation
that each time I stop the girl next door to share a
thought about the world or the weather or the colour of
her hair
I see her shiver with the fear I might keep her there
that I've begun to talk back to the man on the box
that people will look through me at a bus stop
or imagine that I'm deaf when I'm not
I have a place
beyond a room like a battery hen
beyond the Miser Rate
I have a role behind the shrugging of the curtain
that I am a history, actually,
an archive
and a measurement of change
I am not a good cause
nor a tragedy
nor a charity
though sometimes I wish I were a Whale

a bloody great Whale
marooned on our road
so you would notice me

One Spring
when I was nineteen
I swam at midnight without clothes on
with my red hair all splayed out
my beautiful red hair
and a man was there
That was Tuesday
now it's Sunday
quite natural
like the seasons
like the air . . .
(*She pauses, looks at us.*)

The camera pulls out and out and out leaving an old
woman in a room at a window across a street getting
smaller and smaller.

Methuen Contemporary Dramatists
include

Peter Barnes (three volumes)
Sebastian Barry
Edward Bond (six volumes)
Howard Brenton
  (two volumes)
Richard Cameron
Jim Cartwright
Caryl Churchill (two volumes)
Sarah Daniels (two volumes)
Nick Darke
David Edgar (three volumes)
Ben Elton
Dario Fo (two volumes)
Michael Frayn (two volumes)
Paul Godfrey
John Guare
Peter Handke
Jonathan Harvey
Declan Hughes
Terry Johnson (two volumes)
Bernard-Marie Koltès
David Lan
Bryony Lavery
Doug Lucie
David Mamet (three volumes)

Martin McDonagh
Duncan McLean
Anthony Minghella
  (two volumes)
Tom Murphy (four volumes)
Phyllis Nagy
Anthony Nielsen
Philip Osment
Louise Page
Joe Penhall
Stephen Poliakoff
  (three volumes)
Christina Reid
Philip Ridley
Willy Russell
Ntozake Shange
Sam Shepard (two volumes)
Wole Soyinka (two volumes)
David Storey (three volumes)
Sue Townsend
Michel Vinaver (two volumes)
Michael Wilcox
David Wood (two volumes)
Victoria Wood

Methuen World Classics
include

Jean Anouilh (two volumes)
John Arden (two volumes)
Arden & D'Arcy
Brendan Behan
Aphra Behn
Bertolt Brecht (six volumes)
Büchner
Bulgakov
Calderón
Čapek
Anton Chekhov
Noël Coward (seven volumes)
Eduardo De Filippo
Max Frisch
John Galsworthy
Gogol
Gorky
Harley Granville Barker
  (two volumes)
Henrik Ibsen (six volumes)
Lorca (three volumes)

Marivaux
Mustapha Matura
David Mercer (two volumes)
Arthur Miller (five volumes)
Molière
Musset
Peter Nichols (two volumes)
Clifford Odets
Joe Orton
A. W. Pinero
Luigi Pirandello
Terence Rattigan
  (two volumes)
W. Somerset Maugham
  (two volumes)
August Strindberg
  (three volumes)
J. M. Synge
Ramón del Valle-Inclán
Frank Wedekind
Oscar Wilde

Methuen Modern Plays
include work by

For a Complete Catalogue of Methuen Drama titles
write to:

Methuen Drama
215 Vauxhall Bridge Road
London SW1V 1EJ